e	o
げ	ご
ぜ	ぞ
で	ど
べ	ぽ
ぺ	ぽ

v/c	a	u	o
ky	きゃ	きゅ	きょ
sh	しゃ	しゅ	しょ
ch	ちゃ	ちゅ	ちょ
ny	にゃ	にゅ	にょ
hy	ひゃ	ひゅ	ひょ

my	みゃ	みゅ	みょ

ry	りゃ	りゅ	りょ

v/c	a	u	o
gy	ぎゃ	ぎゅ	ぎょ
jy	じゃ	じゅ	じょ
dy	ぢゃ	ぢゅ	ぢょ

by	びゃ	びゅ	びょ
py	ぴゃ	ぴゅ	ぴょ

e	o
ゲ	ゴ
ゼ	ゾ
デ	ド
ベ	ボ
ペ	ポ

v/c	a	u	o
ky	キャ	キュ	キョ
sh	シャ	シュ	ショ
ch	チャ	チュ	チョ
ny	ニャ	ニュ	ニョ
hy	ヒャ	ヒュ	ヒョ

my	ミャ	ミュ	ミョ

ry	リャ	リュ	リョ

v/c	a	u	o
gy	ギャ	ギュ	ギョ
jy	ジャ	ジュ	ジョ
dy	ヂャ	ヂュ	ヂョ

by	ビャ	ビュ	ビョ
py	ピャ	ピュ	ピョ

ti	di
ティ	ディ

fa	fo
ファ	フォ

Japanese for Young People I

Student Book

JAPANESE FOR YOUNG PEOPLE

 **Student Book**

Association for Japanese-Language Teaching

KODANSHA INTERNATIONAL
Tokyo • New York • London

The Authors: The Association for Japanese-Language Teaching (AJALT) was recognized as a nonprofit organization by the Ministry of Education in 1977. It was established to meet the practical needs of people who are not necessarily specialists on Japan but who wish to communicate effectively in Japanese. In 1992 the Association was awarded the Japan Foundation Special Prize.

The Association maintains a web site on the Internet at www. ajalt.org and can be contacted over the Internet via info@ajalt.org by teachers and students who have questions about this textbook or any of the Association's other publications.

Layout and design by Point & Line
All illustrations by Hidemi Makino

Distributed in the United States by Kodansha America, LLC, and in the United Kingdom and continental Europe by Kodansha Europe Ltd.

Published by Kodansha International Ltd., 17–14 Otowa 1-chome, Bunkyo-ku, Tokyo 112–8652.

First Edition, 1998
20 19 18 17 16 15 14 13 12 11 10 09   20 19 18 17 16 15 14 13 12

www.kodansha-intl.com

C
O
N
T
E
N
T
S

CONTENTS

Lesson ❶ INTRODUCTION わたしは バードです。

Functions	Situations	Structures, Expressions, & Vocabulary Sets
INTRODUCTIONS •Meeting for the first time	school	NOUNS 　names　page 7 　countries　page 7 　numbers (0-10)　page 7 　occupations　page 10 「はじめまして」「どうぞ よろしく」 「〜さん」「〜くん」「〜せんせい」

Lesson ❷ TELEPHONE NUMBERS これは がっこうの でんわばんごうです。

Functions	Situations	Structures, Expressions, & Vocabulary Sets
•Asking and giving telephone numbers •Saying please and thank you •Possession	school	NOUNS 　everyday objects　page 19 　numbers (11-20)　page 19 「どうぞ」 「ありがとうございます」

Lesson ❸ TIME いま なんじですか。

Functions	Situations	Structures, Expressions, & Vocabulary Sets
•Asking the time •Telling the time •Starting a conversation •Showing hesitation	school	NOUNS 　time　page 31 　stores　page 31 　activities　page 31 　numbers (10-100)　page 31 「すみません、〜」「ええと、〜」 「どうも ありがとうございました」 「どう いたしまして」

Lesson ❹ DAYS OF THE WEEK きょうは にちようびです。

Functions	Situations	Structures, Expressions, & Vocabulary Sets
•Asking and giving the days of the week •Answering a rollcall •Saying sorry	school home	NOUNS 　days of the week　page 43 　schools subjects　page 43 　numbers (100-1000)　page 43 「すみません」 「ごめんなさい」

Lesson ❺ MONTHS, DAYS OF THE MONTH きのうは あねの たんじょうびでした。

Functions	Situations	Structures, Expressions, & Vocabulary Sets
•Asking and giving ages •Asking and giving dates •Explaining one's family •Cautions •Asking welfare and assuring safety	school	NOUNS 　family　page 53 　months　page 53 　days of the month　page 53 「あぶない」「だいじょうぶ」 COUNTERS　ひとり ふたり 「〜にん」　page 58 SUMMARY TABLE　です　page 57

Lesson 6 — HOW MUCH? それは　いくらですか。

Functions	Situations	Structures, Expressions, & Vocabulary Sets
SHOPPING •Asking and giving the prices of goods •Requesting things •Saying please •Indicating decisions	stationery store	NOUNS 　stationery　　page 71 「いらっしゃいませ」 「〜（を）〜ください」 「みせてください」 「どうぞ」 「じゃあ」

Lesson 7 — COUNTING OBJECTS その　りんごを　みっつください。

Functions	Situations	Structures, Expressions, & Vocabulary Sets
COUNTING •Requesting things •Asking country of manufacture •Spatial location	stationery store bakery	DEMONSTRATIVES NOUNS 　clothes　　page 87 　food　　page 87 　countries　　page 87 　numbers (1,000-100,000)　　page 87 COUNTERS 　「〜つ」「〜ほん」「〜まい」　　page 86 SUMMARY TABLE 　こーそーあーど　　page 81

Lesson 8 — AT A HAMBURGER SHOP おおきい　ポテトを　ください。

Functions	Situations	Structures, Expressions, & Vocabulary Sets
SHOPPING •Requesting things **COUNTING** •Describing things	fast food restaurant coffee shop school	NOUNS 　food　　page 99 –I ADJECTIVES 　colors　　page 99 「おまちください」

Lesson 9 — A FAMOUS TEMPLE これは　ゆうめいな　おてらです。

Functions	Situations	Structures, Expressions, & Vocabulary Sets
•Describing things •Offering and accepting things	home visiting	NOUNS 　places　　page 111 –NA ADJECTIVES　　page 111 「〜は　いかがですか」 「いただきます」

Lesson 10 — THE WEEKEND あした　えいがを　みます。

Functions	Situations	Structures, Expressions, & Vocabulary Sets
•Intentions •Habitual actions	school home	NOUNS 　activities　　page 128 　food　　page 128 ADJECTIVES　　page 128 VERBS　　page 128 ADVERBS OF FREQUENCY　　page 128

Series Guide to
JAPANESE FOR YOUNG PEOPLE

JAPANESE FOR YOUNG PEOPLE is a new three-level series (with an optional starter level for elementary students) designed primarily for junior-high and high school curricula encouraging systematic Japanese-language acquisition through an enjoyable but structured learning process.

Starter Level

Level 1

Japanese for Young People I: Student Book

This first main text in the series introduces basic structures.

Japanese for Young People I: Kana Workbook

A workbook to practice reading and writing the hiragana and katakana native scripts with crossword puzzles, wordsearches and other games that will encourage enjoyable and effective language acquisition.

Level 2

Japanese for Young People II: Student Book

The second main text in the series introduces the conjugation of adjectives and some basic kanji.

Japanese for Young People II: Kanji Workbook

A workbook to practice reading and writing the 70 Chinese characters introduced in the STUDENT BOOK.

Level 3

Japanese for Young People III: Student Book

The third main text in the series introduces verb conjugation and some functional expressions for making requests and asking permission.

Japanese for Young People III: Kanji Workbook

A workbook to practice reading and writing the 80 Chinese characters introduced in the STUDENT BOOK.

Japanese for Young People: Sound & Rhythm

Based on Total Physical Response, this optional level recommended for use by elementary students, encourages pupils to develop essential aural skills by simply listening and following the instructions on the tape. Facilitates smooth progression to Level 1 through familiarization with basic Japanese sounds and words.

Japanese for Young People: Sound & Rhythm Cassette Tapes

Tapes provide essential aural practice through professional recordings from the text.

Japanese for Young People I: Cassette Tapes

Essential aural practice of natural spoken Japanese is facilitated by recordings of marked sections from the STUDENT BOOK and KANA WORKBOOK.

Japanese for Young People I: Teacher's Book

A step-by-step guide in English for instructors of Japanese with suggested games and activities.

Japanese for Young People II: Cassette Tapes

Essential aural practice of natural spoken Japanese is facilitated by recordings of marked sections from the STUDENT BOOK and KANJI WORKBOOK.

Japanese for Young People II: Teacher's Book

A step-by-step guide in English for instructors of Japanese with suggested games and activities.

Japanese for Young People III: Cassette Tapes

Essential aural practice of natural spoken Japanese is facilitated by recordings of marked sections from the STUDENT BOOK and KANJI WORKBOOK.

Japanese for Young People III: Teacher's Book

A step-by-step guide in English for instructors of Japanese with suggested games and activities.

Learners who complete all levels in this series will have covered one third of the grammatical structures needed for beginner Japanese.

A Note to the Teacher

The Characters

All the characters that appear in JAPANESE FOR YOUNG PEOPLE were specially created and developed with particular emphasis on the kind of situations that target learners are likely to encounter in their daily lives at home and school.

The main protagonist is Mike Bird, a thirteen-year-old American boy who is participating in a student exchange program in Japan. He is living with a representative Japanese family, the Katos, and attends a typical Japanese junior-high school.

The Kato family comprises Ken Kato, a boy of the same age as Mike who goes to the same school, Ken's mother and father, and five-year-old sister, Midori. At school Mike makes other friends such as Akira Yamamoto and Sachiko Kimura. He often goes around to Akira's house to play and sometimes meets his mother. Mike's home room teacher is Ms. Keiko Tanaka. Toward the end of this book a senior from the school Judo club also puts in an appearance.

This collection of protagonists which includes friends of the same age, friends' parents, teachers and seniors reflects the fact that this course has been specially designed to facilitate learners' understanding of how Japanese speech levels depend on interpersonal relationships.

The Plain Style

An important characteristic of the Japanese language is that speech levels change according to whom one is speaking to. Factors such as age, position, or rank most often influence the level of speech in Japanese. This series has adopted a specific policy of familiarizing learners with the different usages of the polite and plain styles from the earliest stages because young people are likely to come across the plain style more often than the polite style in their linguistic experiences. A dialogue written in the plain style first appears in Lesson 2 of this book. In order not to hinder the acquisition of grammatical structures at this introductory stage, however, throughout the series we decided against any particle omission simply in the pursuit of reproducing natural Japanese. Similarly, sentence endings are always neutral and no examples of the different endings used by male and female speakers have been included in this book. To start with, the plain style is introduced as something that learners should be able to recognize and understand, but in JAPANESE FOR YOUNG PEOPLE III: STUDENT BOOK it is presented as a structure to be learned alongside the plain form of Japanese verbs.

Script

The native Japanese phonetic scripts, hiragana and katakana, are introduced from the earliest stages of JAPANESE FOR YOUNG PEOPLE I: STUDENT BOOK. Learners, however, are not necessarily required to have mastered native script before starting this book: It has been designed to be used in tandem with JAPANESE FOR YOUNG PEOPLE I: KANA WORKBOOK. To make this possible, romanized Japanese has been included as an auxiliary reading aid for all native script found from Lessons 1 through 5, for Key Sentences and Vocabulary from Lessons 6 through 10, and for Vocabulary from Lessons 11 through 15. All new words are presented in the Vocabulary sections in kana and romanized Japanese with English equivalents.

Ideally learners should be exposed to the full set of hiragana characters by the time they reach Lesson 5.

Length of Course

As a rule each lesson should take approximately four hours of classroom time to complete and accordingly this book can form a sixty-hour classroom-based course. Learners who are familiar with spoken Japanese after using JAPANESE FOR YOUNG PEOPLE: SOUND & RHYTHM or have already mastered the kana scripts will require less time to complete this book.

Vocabulary

JAPANESE FOR YOUNG PEOPLE I: STUDENT BOOK introduces a total of approximately 450 new words including 28 verbs and 21 adjectives.

Audio Tapes

A set of cassette tapes to accompany this course is available separately and is particularly recommended for review and in learning environments with limited access to natural spoken Japanese by native speakers. Unlike many cassette tapes, not all the contents of this book has been recorded. As a guide a tape icon indicates all sections recorded on the tapes. In the Quiz sections this icon indicates that answers are also provided on the tape; a half-tape icon is used when only the question is recorded.

Structure of
JAPANESE FOR YOUNG PEOPLE I: STUDENT BOOK

At the front of this book learners will find an Introduction to the Characters that appear in the lessons and two special preparation activities to help them get started. The core of this first main text comprises fifteen lessons. At the back of the book there is a Grammar Review that summarizes important grammatical information and vocabulary introduced in this volume and a Mini Dictionary that contains three glossaries—Japanese–English with kana lookup, Japanese–English with romaji lookup, and English–Japanese. Both endpapers also provide useful information for all learners. A full and detailed table of the hiragana and katakana scripts has been printed at the front and an annotated map of Japan has been printed at the back.

Sound and Rhythm

An introduction to Japanese phonetics, this section exposes learners to the characteristic sounds— voiced consonants, long vowels, the assimilated sound represented by the small っ, and the sound of the kana ん—and rhythm of Japanese. With examples that include foreign loan words, the aim of this section is to make learners aware that rhythm is different in English and Japanese.

Useful Expressions

Also effective for learning common greetings and salutations, this section is an important introduction to the different levels of speech used in Japanese. For each phrase or expression, two appropriate patterns are presented: One that can be used with friends and the other with elders or seniors. More important than learning each greeting, the aim of this section is to make learners aware that Japanese expressions change according to whom one is speaking to.

The Lessons

The following table shows in detail the structure that forms the core of this book.

Lesson	Function	Situation	Structures, Expressions, & Vocabulary Sets
L1~5	INTRODUCTIONS *school* Meeting for the first time Asking/giving telephone numbers, the time, the days of the week, dates, and ages Starting a conversation Saying please and thank you Saying sorry Asking for confirmation Answering a rollcall		Nouns NUMBERS (0–1000)
L6~8	SHOPPING *stationery store* *coffee shop* Requests & orders Counting things		DEMONSTRATIVES こそあど 「～を（～）ください」 NUMBERS (1000–) COUNTERS（～つ、～円、～枚、～本）
L8~9	DESCRIBING THINGS 1 *homestay family* Offering and accepting tea and cake		ADJECTIVES 1 (MODIFYING) －い／－な ADJECTIVES
L10~11	Intentions, habitual actions, *school* completed actions, past		VERBS 1 (MOTION) ADVERBS OF FREQUENCY
L12~14	COMING & GOING *school* Visiting someone *homestay family* Going out and coming back		VERBS 1 (DIRECTION)
L15	(READING REVIEW)		「～の前に～。」「～の後で～。」

Grammar Review

Organized into Sentence Patterns, Interrogatives, Verbs & Adjectives, and Particles, the Grammar Review summarizes the key grammatical structures and vocabulary sets presented in this book.

Mini Dictionary

A full set of glossaries is included in this volume to facilitate self-study and provide all learners with an opportunity to familiarize themselves with using a bilingual dictionary at this preparatory stage. Both a Japanese–English glossary and an English–Japanese glossary are provided so learners can look up English and Japanese words. Further, both kana and romaji lookup systems are used in the Japanese–English glossary to allow even those not yet familiar with kana to use this dictionary. Indeed the fact that romanized Japanese is used in the Vocabulary sections throughout this volume demonstrates the importance that is placed on self-study.

Lesson Structure

Key Sentences

As an indication of the basic learning objectives of each lesson, the principal sentence patterns are presented as example sentences on the first page of that lesson. Romanized Japanese has been printed alongside the native script from Lessons 1 through 10, so that even at this stage learners will have a general idea of what is contained in any lesson at a glance.

Exercises

All the Exercises in this volume are composed of full color illustrations and cues or examples in Japanese so that learner progress is not impeded by the mundane task of always having to translate from one language into the other. The first exercises in any lesson introduce key vocabulary necessary to practice the sentence patterns. Thereafter the exercises progress at a realistic pace that facilitates practice in spoken Japanese from simple to more complicated sentences. Romanized Japanese is provided as an auxiliary aid to reading kana only through Lesson 5.

Main Dialogue/Text

This section aims to provide learners with functional and situational examples of how the sentence patterns introduced in that lesson are actually used in context. Because it is crucial that learners have an immediate grasp of the situation being illustrated, each dialogue or text is introduced with a short sentence in English that effectively describes the circumstances of that dialogue. Dialogues are also illustrated with a comic strip that summarizes the key points of the conversation with an appropriate number of frames. The speech bubbles contain some English words and pictures to help learners guess what is being said and can be put to particularly effective use in role-playing situations that are based around the dialogue. Some dialogues end with a brief summary sentence that is indicated with the ☺ mark. These summaries have been designed not only to help learners describe what is going on in the dialogue but also to explain the conversation objectively as a third party. Learners will find this practice useful in the future when they begin to write in Japanese. Romanized Japanese is provided as an auxiliary aid to reading kana only through Lesson 5.

Short Dialogues

Two or three shorter dialogues are included both as applications of usage touched on in the Main Dialogue or as illustrations of usage not taken up in the Main Dialogue. Note that to familiarize learners with the different levels of speech used in Japanese, dialogues presented in the plain style are included from Lesson 2. Romanized Japanese is provided as an auxiliary aid to reading kana only through Lesson 5.

Vocabulary

All new words are presented as they appear after the Key Sentences, Exercises, Main Dialogue/Text, and Short Dialogues sections. Note that the English equivalents provided to enable learners to check meaning and organize vocabulary items are restricted to the meaning and usage of the context in which they appear. Romanized Japanese is provided as an auxiliary aid to reading kana throughout this book.

Summary Table

Although a key feature of this course is indeed the lack of any grammatical explanation or linguistic description of sentence patterns, we recognize the need for learners to understand the language system as they progress through this book. Accordingly important grammatical areas have been summarized in tabular form at the end of the last lesson in which they are presented. Learners will find Summary Tables for こ－そ－あ－ど, です, Verbs, and Relative Time Expressions.

Japan News

In some lessons learners will find a Japan News article that provides important background information about traditional and contemporary Japanese culture in English, recognizing the emphasis that is often placed on acquiring a deeper understanding of the country whose language is being studied.

Task

With the aim of facilitating more flexible practice of sentence patterns and vocabulary, a Task has been included in ten lessons. Some such as Task 1 in Lesson 2 (asking for telephone numbers) and Tasks 4 – 6 in Lessons 6 through 8 (shopping) provide situational and functional practice and others are included to improve reading comprehension skills. Romanized Japanese is provided as an auxiliary aid to reading kana only through Lesson 5.

Quiz

A Quiz is included at the end of each lesson to enable learners to check progress. Romanized Japanese is provided as an auxiliary aid to reading kana only through Lesson 5.

ACKNOWLEDGMENTS

This textbook was written by three AJALT instructors, Sachiko Adachi, Harumi Mizuno, and Mieko Chosho. They were assisted by Sanae Kimu, Mitsuyoshi Kaji, and Hiroshi Higuchi. Special thanks are due to Hidemi Makino who single-handedly created all the illustrations in this textbook. The authors would also like to thank Paul Hulbert and other editorial staff at Kodansha International for translating and compiling the glossaries, as well as the usual editorial tasks.

Preparation of this textbook was partially assisted by a grant from The Foundation of Language Education.

Introducing the Characters

The Bird Family

❶ マイク　バード (13)
Maiku Bādo

An American junior-high school student from Colorado, Mike Bird is living with the Kato family in Tokyo while attending the local school as an exchange student. He is an avid judoist who aims to improve his skills while in Japan.

The Kato Family
❷ かとう　けん (13)
Katō Ken

Ken is Mike Bird's classmate and best friend. He may not be a grade A student but is a popular boy with a capacity to make his schoolfriends laugh. A keen runner and the class clown.

❸ かとう　みどり (5)
Katō Midori

Ken's little sister loves reading manga comics.

❹ かとう　たかし (42)
Katō Takashi

Ken's father is an employee of a large Japanese corporation who spends his free time practicing his golf stroke to impress his clients.

❺ かとう　まさこ (39)
Katō Masako

Ken's mother loves watching video movies.

❻ たなか　けいこ (27)
Tanaka Keiko

Mike Bird's home room teacher is mad about hot springs.

❼ きむら　さちこ (13)
Kimura Sachiko

Mike's classmate likes music.

❽ きむら　たま
Kimura Tama

Sachiko was given her pet cat by her next door neighbor.

❾ やまもと　あきら (13)
Yamamoto Akira

A classmate who has lots of computer games, Yamamoto Akira is bookish and fast on his feet.

❿ せんぱい (15)
sempai

A senior boy at school and member of the Judo club.

⓫ やまもと　じゅんこ (39)
Yamamoto Junko

Yamamoto Akira's mother.

The Bird Family
Their home is in Colorado in the United States of America.

❶ ハリー　バード (48)
Harii Bādo

Mike's father is an attorney at law.

❷ スーザン　バード (45)
Sūzan Bādo

Mike's mother bakes fine apple pie.

❸ ナンシー　バード (17)
Nanshii Bādo

Mike's older sister is a fine singer and a member of the school choir.

❹ ビル　バード (10)
Biru Bādo

Mike's little brother is a budding sportsman.

❺ エリザベス　バード (72)
Erizabesu Bādo

Mike's grandmother lives in New York.

Sound & Rhythm

⑨

⑩

⑪

⑫

⑬

⑭

✪ V O C A B U L A R Y ✪

トマト	tomato	tomato
バナナ	banana	banana
みかん	mandarin orange, satsuma	mikan
りんご	apple	ringo
ケーキ	cake	kēki
チョコレート	chocolate	chokorēto
ほん	book	hon
えんぴつ	pencil	empitsu
きって	stamp	kitte
ざっし	magazine	zasshi
サッカー	soccer	sakka
じゅうどう	judo	jūdō
すきやき	sukiyaki	sukiyaki
てんぷら	tempura	tempura

Useful Expressions

①

②

③

④

a.

b.

⑤

a.

b.

⑥

a.

b.

⑦

a.

b.

⑧

⑨

Lesson 1

INTRODUCTION

わたしは バードです。

KEY SENTENCES

1. わたしは バードです。

2. わたしは せんせいではありません。

3. バードくんは アメリカじんですか。

4. わたしは たなかせんせいの せいとです。

1. Watashi wa Bādo desu.
2. Watashi wa sensē dewa arimasen.
3. Bādo-kun wa Amerika-jin desu ka.
4. Watashi wa Tanaka-sensē no sēto desu.

☆VOCABULARY☆

わたし	I	watashi
は	as for (topic marker, particle)	wa
バード	Bird (surname)	Bādo
です	is, will be (See SUMMARY TABLE on p.57)	desu
バードくん	(Mr.) Bird	Bādo-kun
〜くん	(suffix) (See NOTE)	-kun
アメリカじん	an American (person)	Amerika-jin
アメリカ	America	Amerika
〜じん	person (suffix)	-jin
か	=? (question marker, particle)	ka
せんせい	teacher	sensē
ではありません	is not, will not be (See SUMMARY TABLE on p.57)	dewa arimasen
たなかせんせい	Ms.Tanaka (surname with honorific for a teacher)	Tanaka-sensē
〜せんせい	(suffix for a teacher)	-sensē
の	='s (possessive particle)	no
せいと	student, pupil	sēto

 The suffix -kun is less polite than -san and is mainly used when addressing younger men or boys. It is never used between women or when addressing elders.

EXERCISES I

1. **a. ex.** バード　Bādo

   b. ex. マイク　Maiku

   c. ex. マイク　バード　Maiku Bādo

2. **a. ex.** バードくんです。　Bādo-kun desu.

   b. ex. マイクくんです。　Maiku-kun desu.

   c. ex. マイク　バードくんです。　Maiku Bādo-kun desu.

ex.

①　②　③　④

EXERCISES II

ex.

1. **ex.** にほん　Nihon

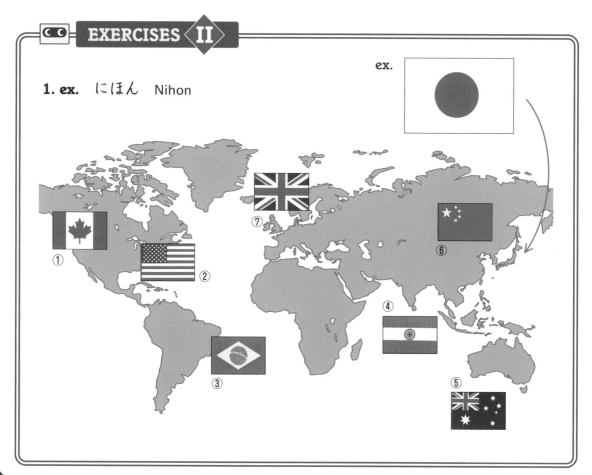

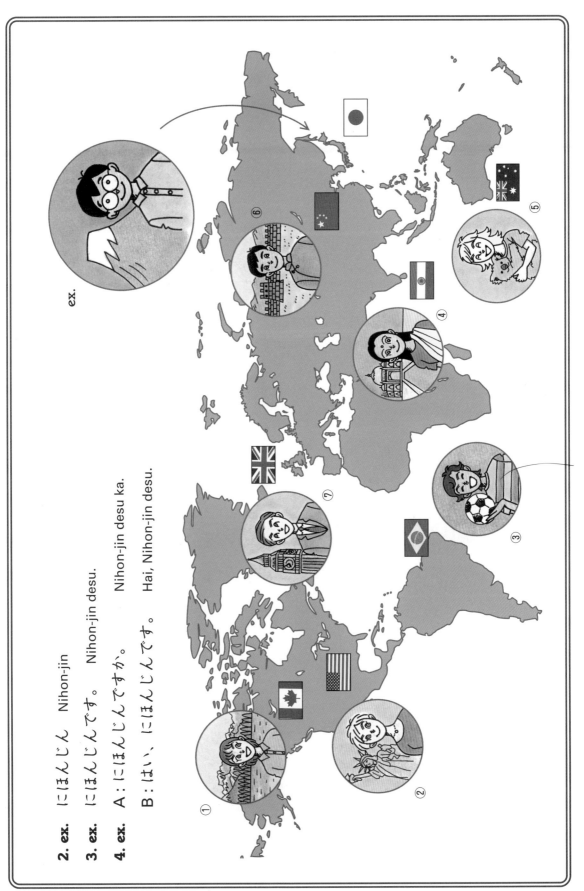

2. ex. にほんじん Nihon-jin

3. ex. にほんじんです。 Nihon-jin desu.

4. ex. A : にほんじんですか。 Nihon-jin desu ka.

　　　　B : はい、にほんじんです。 Hai, Nihon-jin desu.

EXERCISES III

ex. A：ちゅうごくじんですか、にほんじんですか。
Chūgoku-jin desu ka, Nihon-jin desu ka.

B：にほんじんです。
Nihon-jin desu.

ex.

②

①

③

④

⑤

⑥

⑦

ex. A : ちゅうごくじんですか。
Chūgoku-jin desu ka.

B : いいえ、ちゅうごくじんではありません。　にほんじんです。
Iie, Chūgoku-jin dewa arimasen.　Nihon-jin desu.

① ②

③

④

⑦

EXERCISES V

1. ex. せんせい　　sensē

2. ex. a. たなかせんせいは　バードくんの　せんせいです。

Tanaka-sensē wa Bādo-kun no sensē desu.

b. バードくんは　たなかせんせいの　せいとです。

Bādo-kun wa Tanaka-sensē no sēto desu.

⭐ V O C A B U L A R Y ⭐

かとう	Kato (surname)	Katō
きむら	Kimura (surname)	Kimura
マイク	Mike (given name)	Maiku
ナンシー	Nancy (given name)	Nanshii
けん	Ken (given name)	Ken
さちこ	Sachiko (given name)	Sachiko
けいこ	Keiko (given name)	Kēko
バードさん	Miss Bird (surname with honorific suffix)	Bādo-san
〜さん	Mr., Mrs., Ms., Miss (honorific suffix)	-san
にほん	Japan	Nihon
カナダ	Canada	Kanada
ブラジル	Brazil	Burajiru
インド	India	Indo
オーストラリア	Australia	Ōsutoraria
ちゅうごく	China	Chūgoku
イギリス	England	Igirisu
ともだち	friend	tomodachi
はい	yes	hai
いいえ	no	iie

NUMBERS From 0 to 10

0	ゼロ、れい	zero, rei
1	いち	ichi
2	に	ni
3	さん	san
4	よん、し	yon, shi
5	ご	go
6	ろく	roku
7	なな、しち	nana, shichi
8	はち	hachi
9	きゅう、く	kyū, ku
10	じゅう	jū

MAIN DIALOGUE

The principal introduces Bādo-kun to Tanaka-sensē.

こうちょうせんせい：たなかせんせい、マイク　バードくんです。

バードくん　　　　　：はじめまして。　バードです。

たなかせんせい　　　：はじめまして。　たなかです。

こうちょうせんせい：バードくん、たなかせんせいは　バードくんの
　　　　　　　　　　　せんせいです。

バードくん　　　　　：どうぞ　よろしく。

たなかせんせい　　　：どうぞ　よろしく。

☺バードくんは　たなかせんせいの　せいとです。

Kōchō-sensē　 :　Tanaka-sensē, Maiku Bādo-kun desu.
Bādo-kun　　　:　Hajimemashite. Bādo desu.
Tanaka-sensē :　Hajimemashite. Tanaka desu.
Kōchō-sensē　 :　Bādo-kun, Tanaka-sensē wa Bādo-kun no sensē desu.
Bādo-kun　　　:　Dōzo yoroshiku.
Tanaka-sensē :　Dōzo yoroshiku.

☺ Bādo-kun wa Tanaka-sensē no sēto desu.

VOCABULARY

こうちょう	principal	kōchō
はじめまして	How do you do?	hajimemashite
バードくんの	your	Bādo-kun no
どうぞ　よろしく	I'm very glad to meet you.	dōzo yoroshiku

SHORT DIALOGUES

1

たなかせんせい：バードくんの　おとうさんは
　　　　　　　　かいしゃいんですか。
バードくん　　：いいえ、かいしゃいんではありません。
　　　　　　　　べんごしです。

Tanaka-sensē : Bādo-kun no otōsan wa kaisha-in desu ka.
Bādo-kun　　 : Iie, kaisha-in dewa arimasen.
　　　　　　　　Bengoshi desu.

2

せんせい　　　：バードくんは　アメリカじんですか、
　　　　　　　　オーストラリアじんですか。
バードくん　　：アメリカじんです。

Sensē　　 : Bādo-kun wa Amerika-jin desu ka, Ōsutoraria-jin desu ka.
Bādo-kun : Amerika-jin desu.

VOCABULARY

おとうさん	father	otōsan
かいしゃいん	company employee	kaisha-in
べんごし	lawyer	bengoshi

QUIZ

I. Make sentences as shown in the example.

ex.  → <u>にほんじんです。</u>

<u>Nihon-jin desu.</u>

1. → _____

2.  → _____

3. → _____

4. → _____

5. → _____

QUIZ

[cc]

II. Make sentences as shown in the example.

ex.　バードくん・せいと

Bādo-kun • sēto

→バードくんは　せいとです。

Bādo-kun wa sēto desu.

1.　けんくん・せいと

Ken-kun • sēto

→ _____

2.　たなかさん・せんせい

Tanaka-san • sensē

→ _____

3.　かとうくん・バードくんの　ともだち

Katō-kun • Bādo-kun no tomodachi

→ _____

[cc]

III. Answer the questions below as shown in the example.

ex.　バードくんは　アメリカじんですか。

Bādo-kun wa Amerika-jin desu ka.

→はい、アメリカじんです。

Hai, Amerika-jin desu.

ナンシーさんは　インドじんですか。

Nanshii-san wa Indo-jin desu ka.

→いいえ、インドじんではありません。

　Iie, Indo-jin dewa arimasen.

1. ナンシーさんは　アメリカじんですか。

Nanshii-san wa Amerika-jin desu ka.

→

_____

2. きむらさんは　ちゅうごくじんですか。

Kimura-san wa Chūgoku-jin desu ka.

→

_____

3. バードくんの　おとうさんは　せんせいですか。

Bādo-kun no otōsan wa sensē desu ka.

→

_____

4. バードくんの　おとうさんは　べんごしですか。

Bādo-kun no otōsan wa bengoshi desu ka.

→

_____

IV. Match the number to the correct word as shown in the example.

ex.   **1**·   ·さん   san

1.   **2**·   ·に   ni

2.   **3**·   ·はち   hachi

3.   **4**·   ·ろく   roku

4.   **5**·   ·よん、し   yon, shi

5.   **6**·   ·いち   ichi

6.   **7**·   ·じゅう   jū

7.   **8**·   ·ご   go

8.   **9**·   ·きゅう、く   kyū, ku

9.   **10**·   ·なな、しち   nana, shichi

これは　がっこうの　でんわばんごうです。

KEY SENTENCES

1. これは　ほんです。

2. これは　ほんではありません。

3. これは　たなかせんせいの　とけいです。

   これは　たなかせんせいのです。

4. がっこうの　でんわばんごうは

   3785−2411です。

1. Kore wa hon desu.
2. Kore wa hon dewa arimasen.
3. Kore wa Tanaka-sensē no tokē desu.
   Kore wa Tanaka-sensē no desu.
4. Gakkō no denwa-bangō wa san-nana-hachi-go no ni-yon-ichi-ichi desu.

☆ VOCABULARY ☆

これ	this	kore
とけい	watch, clock	tokē
たなかせんせいのです	It's Ms.Tanaka's.	Tanaka-sensē no desu
がっこう	school	gakkō
でんわばんごう	telephone number	denwa-bangō
でんわ	telephone	denwa
ばんごう	number	bangō

EXERCISES I

1. ex. ノート　nōto

ex.

 ① ② ③ ④ ⑤ ⑥ ⑦ ⑧

2. ex. これは　ノートです。　Kore wa nōto desu.

3. ex. A: これは　ノートですか。　Kore wa nōto desu ka.

B: はい、ノートです。　Hai, nōto desu.

4. ex. A: これは　<u>ほん</u>ですか。
Kore wa <u>hon</u> desu ka.

B: いいえ、<u>ほん</u>ではありません。
Iie, <u>hon</u> dewa arimasen.

A: なんですか。
Nan desu ka.

B: <u>ノート</u>です。
<u>Nōto</u> desu.

2,3. ex.

4. ex. book

①
① notebook

②
② newspaper

③
③ car

④
④ bag

⑤
⑤ key

⑥
⑥ chair

⑦
⑦ desk

⑧
⑧ watch

1. ex. これは　バードくんの　ノートです。

Kore wa Bādo-kun no nōto desu.

2. ex. これは　がっこうの　つくえです。

Kore wa gakkō no tsukue desu.

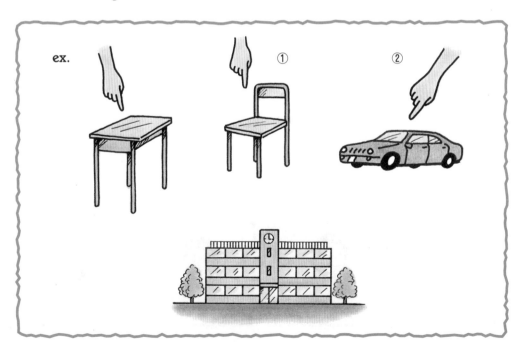

2. ex. A: だれの　ノートですか。　Dare no nōto desu ka.

B: おとうさんのです。　　Otōsan no desu.

ex. <image: notebook>

① <image: にほんのはなし book>

② <image: watch/clock>

③ <image: 新聞 newspaper>

④ <image: keys>

⑤ <image: briefcase>

⑥ <image: car>

<image: faces and building connected by maze lines>

🔊 EXERCISES III

1. ex. がっこう　gakkō

2. ex. がっこうの　でんわばんごうは　3785-2411です。
Gakkō no denwa-bangō wa san-nana-hachi-go no ni-yon-ichi-ichi desu.

3. ex. A: がっこうの　でんわばんごうは
なんばんですか。
Gakkō no denwa-bangō wa nan-ban desu ka.

B: 3785-2411です。
San-nana-hachi-go no ni-yon-ichi-ichi desu.

ex. <image: school building> *3785-2411*

① company
5460-6933

②
3612-8724

③
3550-9245

④
5962-0087

★ V O C A B U L A R Y ★

ノート	notebook	nōto
しんぶん	newspaper	shimbun
かぎ	key	kagi
かばん	bag	kaban
つくえ	desk	tsukue
いす	chair	isu
くるま	car	kuruma
なん	what?	nan
やまもと	Yamamoto (surname)	Yamamoto
だれの	whose	dare no
かいしゃ	company	kaisha
うち	home	uchi
なんばん	what number	nan-ban
～ばん	number (counter)	-ban

11	じゅういち	jūichi
12	じゅうに	jūni
13	じゅうさん	jūsan
14	じゅうよん、じゅうし	jūyon, jūshi
15	じゅうご	jūgo
16	じゅうろく	jūroku
17	じゅうなな、じゅうしち	jūnana, jūshichi
18	じゅうはち	jūhachi
19	じゅうきゅう、じゅうく	jūkyū, jūku
20	にじゅう	nijū

NUMBERS From 11 to 20

MAIN DIALOGUE

**Tanaka-sensē gives Bādo-kun a piece of paper.
Something is written in Kanji on it.**

たなかせんせい： バードくん、どうぞ。

バードくん　　　： ありがとうございます。

　　　　　　　　　これは　がっこうの　でんわばんごうですか。

たなかせんせい： はい。 3785-2411です。

バードくん　　　： これは？

たなかせんせい： わたしの　なまえです。　たなか　けいこです。

☺ がっこうの　でんわばんごうは　3785-2411です。

　　バードくんの　せんせいの　なまえは　たなか　けいこです。

Tanaka-sensē:　Bādo-kun, dōzo.
Bādo-kun　　 :　Arigatō gozaimasu.
　　　　　　　　Kore wa gakkō no denwa-bangō desu ka.
Tanaka-sensē:　Hai. San-nana-hachi-go no ni-yon-ichi-ichi desu.
Bādo-kun　　 :　Kore wa?
Tanaka-sensē:　Watashi no namae desu. Tanaka Kēko desu.

☺ Gakkō no denwa-bangō wa san-nana-hachi-go no ni-yon-ichi-ichi desu.
　 Bādo-kun no sensē no namae wa Tanaka Kēko desu.

VOCABULARY

わたしの	my	watashi no
これは？	as for this?	kore wa?
なまえ	name	namae

東京中学校

3785 – 2411

田中 恵子

SHORT DIALOGUES

1

バードくん　：せんせいの　うちの　でんわばんごうは
　　　　　　　　　なんばんですか。

せんせい　　：３６１２−８７２４です。

バードくん　：やまもとくんの　うちの　でんわばんごうは？

せんせい　　：ちょっと　まってください。　３５５０−９２４６です。

Bādo-kun　：　Sensē no uchi no denwa-bangō wa nan-ban desu ka.
Sensē　　　：　San-roku-ichi-ni no hachi-nana-ni-yon desu.
Bādo-kun　：　Yamamoto-kun no uchi no denwa-bangō wa?
Sensē　　　：　Chotto matte kudasai. San-go-go-zero no kyu-ni-yon-roku desu.

2

バードくん　：これは　なに。

かとうくん　：そろばん。

バードくん　：かとうくんの？

かとうくん　：うん、ぼくの。

Bādo-kun　：　Kore wa nani.
Katō-kun　：　Soroban.
Bādo-kun　：　Katō-kun no?
Katō-kun　：　Un, boku no.

JAPAN NEWS

A soroban is a Japanese abacus. Children are taught how to do sums on the soroban at elementary school or even in special private classes that offer more focused soroban instruction.

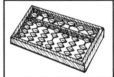

A Soroban

Many shopkeepers can do their sums with a soroban quicker than a pocket calculator. Regular use of a soroban can actually improve your mental arithmetic.

Competitions are often held throughout Japan where skilled soroban operators challenge computers in a race to find the fastest calculator. Believe it or not, the soroban usually wins.

VOCABULARY

なに	what	nani
そろばん	abacus	soroban
うん	um, un-huh, yeah (informal)	un
ぼく	I (informal male speech)	boku

T A S K ①

でんわばんごうは　なんばんですか。

Find out your friends' phone numbers and write them in the chart.

ex.

バードくん：　<u>スミスさん</u>の　うちの　でんわばんごうは
　　　　　　　なんばんですか。

スミスさん：　<u>０３－３４５９－９６２０</u>です。

バードくん：　すみません*¹、もういちど　おねがいします。*²

スミスさん：　<u>０３－３４５９－９６２０</u>です。

バードくん：　<u>０３－３４５９－９６２０</u>ですね。*³

スミスさん：　はい、そうです。

バードくん：　ありがとうございます。

Bādo-kun　：　Sumisu-san no uchi no denwa-bangō wa nan-ban desu ka.
Sumisu-san:　Zero-san no san-yon-go-kyū no kyū-roku-ni-zero desu.
Bādo-kun　：　Sumimasen,*¹ mō ichido onegai shimasu.*²
Sumisu-san:　Zero-san no san-yon-go-kyū no kyū-roku-ni-zero desu.
Bādo-kun　：　Zero-san no san-yon-go-kyū no kyū-roku-ni-zero desu ne.*³
Sumisu-san:　Hai, sō desu.
Bādo-kun　：　Arigatō gozaimasu.

*¹すみません	Pardon me　　Sumimasen
*²もういちど　おねがいします	Please repeat it　Mō ichido onegai shimasu
*³ね	Isn't it? (particle)　-ne

	なまえ	でんわばんごう
ex.	ス ミ ス ⓢⓝくん	03-3459-9620
1	さん/くん	
2	さん/くん	
3	さん/くん	
4	さん/くん	
5	さん/くん	

CC

I. Put the appropriate particles in the parentheses.

1. これ（　　　）バードくん（　　　）ノートです。

Kore ( ) Bādo-kun ( ) nōto desu.

2. これ（　　　）せんせい（　　　）かばんです。

Kore ( ) sensē ( ) kaban desu.

3. がっこう（　　　）でんわばんごう（　　　）3785−2411です。

Gakkō ( ) denwa-bangō ( ) san-nana-hachi-go no ni-yon-ichi-ichi desu.

CC

II. Complete the questions so that they fit the answers.

1. A：これは　（　　　　　　）の　かぎですか。

　　Kore wa (　　　) no kagi desu ka.

　B：はい、せんせいのです。

　　Hai, sensē no desu.

2. A：これは　（　　　　　　）の　しんぶんですか。

　　Kore wa (　　　) no shimbun desu ka.

　B：いいえ、きむらさんのではありません。　わたしのです。

　　Iie, Kimura-san no dewa arimasen.　Watashi no desu.

3. A：これは　（　　　　　　）の　ほんですか。

Kore wa (　　　) no hon desu ka.

B：わたしのです。

Watashi no desu.

4. A：やまもとくんの　うちの　でんわばんごうは

（　　　　　　）ですか。

Yamamoto-kun no uchi no denwa-bangō wa (　　　) desu ka.

B：3550−9246です。

San-go-go-zero no kyū-ni-yon-roku desu.

III. Answer the following questions.

1. おとうさんは　かいしゃいんですか。

Otōsan wa kaisha-in desu ka.

→ _____

2. うちの　でんわばんごうは　なんばんですか。

Uchi no denwa-bangō wa nan-ban desu ka.

→ _____

ex. **11** ·⟍   · じゅうご　　　jūgo

1. **12** ·　　　　⟍   · じゅうなな　　jūnana
　　　　　　　　　⟍　　　　じゅうしち　　jūshichi

2. **13** ·　　　　　　　　⟍   · じゅういち　　jūichi

3. **14** ·   · じゅうよん　　jūyon
　　　　　　　　　　　　　　じゅうし　　　jūshi

4. **15** ·   · にじゅう　　　nijū

5. **16** ·   · じゅうに　　　jūni

6. **17** ·   · じゅうきゅう　jūkyū
　　　　　　　　　　　　　　じゅうく　　　jūku

7. **18** ·   · じゅうろく　　jūroku

8. **19** ·   · じゅうさん　　jūsan

9. **20** ·   · じゅうはち　　jūhachi

いま　なんじですか。

KEY SENTENCES

1. いま　8じです。

2. ひるやすみは　12じはんから　1じはんまでです。

8じです。

1. Ima hachi-ji desu.

2. Hiru-yasumi wa jūni-ji han kara
   ichi-ji han made desu.

VOCABULARY

いま	now	ima
8じ	8 o'clock	hachi-ji
〜じ	o'clock	-ji
ひるやすみ	lunch time	hiru-yasumi
ひる	noon	hiru
やすみ	rest (period)	yasumi
12じはん	half past twelve (lit. twelve o'clock half)	jūni-ji han
〜はん	half	-han
から	from (particle)	kara
まで	until (particle)	made

EXERCISES **I**

1. **a. ex.** いちじ　ichi-ji　　　　　　**ex.** | 1:00 |

① 2:00 ② 3:00 ③ 4:00 ④ 5:00

⑤ 6:00 ⑥ 7:00 ⑦ 8:00 ⑧ 9:00

⑨ 10:00 ⑩ 11:00 ⑪ 12:00

b. ex. いちじはん　ichi-ji han

c. ex. くじ　ごふん　ku-ji go-fun

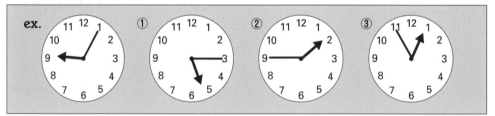

d. ex. よじ　じゅっぷん　yo-ji juppun

e. ex. ごぜん　しちじ　gozen shichi-ji

2. ex. いま　7じです。　　Ima shichi-ji desu.

3. ex. A：いま　なんじですか。

B：7じです。

A：Ima nan-ji desu ka.

B：Shichi-ji desu.

ex.

①

②

③

④

⑤

⑥

⑦

⑧

⑨

EXERCISES II

1. ex. 7じから　11じまでです。

Shichi-ji kara jūichi-ji made desu.

2. ex. A：なんじからですか。

B：7じからです。

A：Nan-ji kara desu ka.

B：Shichi-ji kara desu.

3. ex. A：なんじまでですか。

B：11じまでです。

A：Nan-ji made desu ka.

B：Jūichi-ji made desu.

4. ex. A：なんじから　なんじまでですか。

B：7じから　11じまでです。

A：Nan-ji kara nan-ji made desu ka.

B：Shichi-ji kara jūichi-ji made desu.

ex.

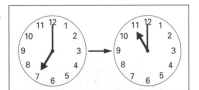

①

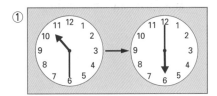

②

③

EXERCISES III

1. ex.　スーパー　sūpā

2. ex.　スーパーは　7じから　11じまでです。
Sūpā wa shichi-ji kara jūichi-ji made desu.

3. ex.　A：スーパーは　なんじからですか。

　　　　B：7じからです。

　　　A：Sūpā wa nan-ji kara desu ka.
　　　B：Shichi-ji kara desu.

ex.

7:00 −11:00

4. ex.　A：スーパーは　なんじまでですか。

　　　　B：11じまでです。

　　　A：Sūpā wa nan-ji made desu ka.
　　　B：Jūichi-ji made desu.

5. ex.　A：スーパーは　なんじから　なんじまでですか。

　　　　B：7じから　11じまでです。

　　　A：Sūpā wa nan-ji kara nan-ji made desu ka.
　　　B：Shichi-ji kara jūichi-ji made desu.

① 10:00 −6:00

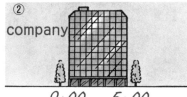

② company 9:00 −5:00

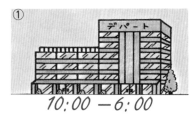

③ 9:00 −7:00

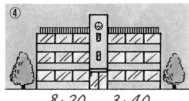

④ 8:20 −3:40

⑤ 8:30 −3:20

⑥ 12:30 −1:30

⑦ 3:20 −3:40

5ふん	5 minutes	go-fun
～ふん	-minutes	-fun
15ふん	15 minutes	jūgo-fun
45ふん	45 minutes	yonjūgo-fun
55ふん	55 minutes	gojūgo-fun
10ぷん	10 minutes	juppun
～ぷん	-minutes	-pun
20ぷん	20 minutes	nijuppun
40ぷん	40 minutes	yonjuppun
50ぷん	50 minutes	gojuppun
ごぜん	AM	gozen
ごご	PM	gogo
なんじ	what time	nan-ji
スーパー	supermarket	sūpā
デパート	department store	depāto
しごと	work	shigoto
べんきょう	study	benkyō
そうじ	cleaning	sōji

TIME

1じ（いちじ）	1 o'clock	ichi-ji
2じ（にじ）	2 o'clock	ni-ji
3じ（さんじ）	3 o'clock	san-ji
4じ（よじ）	4 o'clock	yo-ji
5じ（ごじ）	5 o'clock	go-ji
6じ（ろくじ）	6 o'clock	roku-ji
7じ（しちじ）	7 o'clock	shichi-ji
8じ（はちじ）	8 o'clock	hachi-ji
9じ（くじ）	9 o'clock	ku-ji
10じ（じゅうじ）	10 o'clock	jū-ji
11じ（じゅういちじ）	11 o'clock	jūichi-ji
12じ（じゅうにじ）	12 o'clock	jūni-ji

NUMBERS From 10 to 100

10	じゅう	jū
20	にじゅう	nijū
30	さんじゅう	sanjū
40	よんじゅう	yonjū
50	ごじゅう	gojū
60	ろくじゅう	rokujū
70	ななじゅう	nanajū
80	はちじゅう	hachijū
90	きゅうじゅう	kyūjū
100	ひゃく	hyaku

MAIN DIALOGUE

Bādo-kun asks Tanaka-sensē the time.

バードくん　　　：すみません、いま　なんじですか。

たなかせんせい：8じです。

バードくん　　　：べんきょうは　なんじからですか。

たなかせんせい：8じはんからです。

バードくん　　　：なんじまでですか。

たなかせんせい：3じ20ぷんまでです。

バードくん　　　：どうも　ありがとうございました。

たなかせんせい：どう　いたしまして。

☺ べんきょうは　8じはんから　3じ20ぷんまでです。

Bādo-kun:	Sumimasen, ima nan-ji desu ka.
Tanaka-sensē:	Hachi-ji desu.
Bādo-kun:	Benkyō wa nan-ji kara desu ka.
Tanaka-sensē:	Hachi-ji han kara desu.
Bādo-kun:	Nan-ji made desu ka.
Tanaka-sensē:	San-ji nijuppun made desu.
Bādo-kun:	Dōmo arigatō gozaimashita.
Tanaka-sensē:	Dō itashimashite.

☺ Benkyō wa hachi-ji han kara san-ji nijuppun made desu.

VOCABULARY

すみません	Excuse me. (See NOTE)	sumimasen
どうも　ありがとうございました	Thank you very much.	dōmo arigatō gozaimashita
どう　いたしまして	Don't mention it.	dō itashimahshite
	You're welcome.	
	(lit. What have (I) done?)	

 Sumimasen which you learned in Task 1 on page 23 prefaces a request, such as asking someone for information. It can also mean "Thank you," "I'm sorry," or "Pardon me."

① Excuse me, What time is it now?

② 8:00

③ What time does class start?

④ 8:30–

⑤ . . . . ?

⑥ –3:20

⑦ . . . .

⑧ You are welcome.

SHORT DIALOGUES

1

かとうくん： バードくん、コロラドは いま なんじ。

バードくん： ええと、ごぜん 7じ。

Katō-kun: Bādo-kun, Kororado wa ima nan-ji.
Bādo-kun: Ēto, gozen shichi-ji.

2

かとうくんの おとうさん： ひるやすみは なんじから なんじまで。

バードくん ： 12じはんから 1じはんまでです。

Katō-kun no otōsan: Hiru-yasumi wa nan-ji kara nan-ji made.
Bādo-kun: Jūni-ji han kara ichi-ji han made desu.

VOCABULARY

コロラド	Colorado	Kororado
ええと	Let me see.	ēto

T A S K ❷

とうきょうは いま ごぜん 6じです。

I. What time is it? Using the time differences as a guide, write down the correct time for each city.

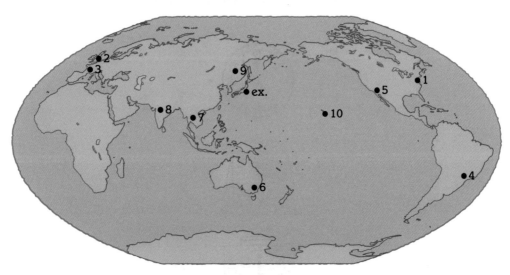

	CITY	TIME DIFFERENCE	TIME
ex.	とうきょう	0 hours	ごぜん 6じ
1	ニューヨーク	-14	ごご 4じ
2	ロンドン	-9	
3	パリ	-8	ごご 10じ
4	サンパウロ	-12	
5	ロサンゼルス	-17	
6	シドニー	+1	
7	バンコク	-2	
8	ニューデリー	-3.5	ごぜん 2じはん
9	ペキン	-1	
10	ホノルル	-19	

II. Using the information in the chart, make statements as in the example.

ex. とうきょうは いま ごぜん 6じです。
Tōkyō wa ima gozen roku-ji desu.

I. Write the time in Hiragana.

ex. 1 (いち) じ   **6.** 7 ( ) じ

1. 2 ( ) じ   **7.** 8 ( ) じ

2. 3 ( ) じ   **8.** 9 ( ) じ

3. 4 ( ) じ   **9.** 10 ( ) じ

4. 5 ( ) じ   **10.** 11 ( ) じ

5. 6 ( ) じ   **11.** 12 ( ) じ

II. Put the appropriate particles in the parentheses.

1. いま　なんじです（　　　）。

Ima nan-ji desu (　　　).

2. がっこう（　　　）8じはん（　　　　　）3じ（　　　　　）です。

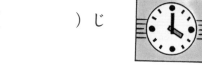

Gakkō (　　　) hachi-ji han (　　　　) san-ji (　　　　) desu.

III. Complete the questions so that they fit the answers.

1.   A : べんきょうは（　　　　　　　　）からですか。
     Benkyō wa (　　　　　) kara desu ka.

     B : はい、8 じからです。
     Hai, hachi-ji kara desu.

2.   A : ひるやすみは（　　　　　　　　）からですか。
     Hiru-yasumi wa (　　　　　) kara desu ka.

     B : いいえ、12 じからではありません。
     Iie, jūni-ji kara dewa arimasen.

3.   A : しごとは（　　　　　　　　）までですか。
     Shigoto wa (　　　　　) made desu ka.

     B : 5 じまでです。
     Go-ji made desu.

4.   A : いま（　　　　　　　　）ですか。
     Ima (　　　　　) desu ka.

     B : 10 じ 20 ぷんです。
     Jū-ji nijuppun desu.

5.   A : デパートは（　　　　　　）から（　　　　　　　　）までですか。
     Depāto wa (　　　　　) kara (　　　　　) made desu ka.

     B : 10 じから　6 じまでです。
     Jū-ji kara roku-ji made desu.

IV. Match the number to the correct word as shown in the example.

ex. よんじゅう yonjū   ·   · **100**

1. ろくじゅう rokujū ·   · **70**

2. にじゅう nijū ·   · **30**

3. きゅうじゅう kyūjū ·   · **50**

4. ひゃく hyaku ·   · **90**

5. さんじゅう sanjū ·   · **40**

6. じゅう jū ·   · **20**

7. ごじゅう gojū ·   · **60**

8. はちじゅう hachijū ·   · **80**

9. ななじゅう nanajū ·   · **10**

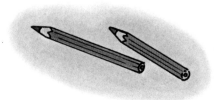

DAYS OF THE WEEK

きょうは　にちようびです。

KEY SENTENCES

1. きょうは　にちようびです。
2. きのうは　どようびでした。
3. きのうは　きんようびではありませんでした。
4. にほんごは　げつようびと　もくようびです。

1. Kyō wa nichi-yōbi desu.
2. Kinō wa dō-yōbi deshita.
3. Kinō wa kin-yōbi dewa arimasendeshita.
4. Nihon-go wa getsu-yōbi to moku-yōbi desu.

VOCABULARY

きょう	today	kyō
にちようび	Sunday	nichi-yōbi
～ようび	day of the week	-yōbi
きのう	yesterday	kinō
どようび	Saturday	do-yōbi
でした	was (See SUMMARY TABLE on p.57)	deshita
きんようび	Friday	kin-yōbi
ではありませんでした	was not (See SUMMARY TABLE on p.57)	dewa arimasendeshita
にほんご	Japanese language	Nihon-go
～ご	language	-go
げつようび	Monday	getsu-yōbi
と	and (particle)	to
もくようび	Thursday	moku-yōbi

EXERCISES **I**

1. a. ex. にちようび　nichi-yōbi

ex.　①　②　③　④　⑤　⑥

b.ex. きょう　kyō

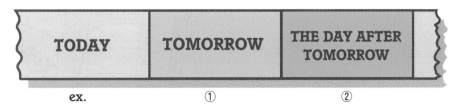

TODAY	TOMORROW	THE DAY AFTER TOMORROW

ex.　①　②

2. ex. きょうは　にちようびです。　Kyō wa nichi-yōbi desu.

3. ex. A : きょうは　げつようびですか。

B : いいえ、げつようびではありません。

A : なんようびですか。

B : にちようびです。

A : Kyō wa getsu-yōbi desu ka.

B : Iie, getsu-yōbi dewa arimasen.

A : Nan-yōbi desu ka.

B : Nichi-yōbi desu.

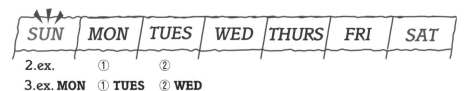

SUN	MON	TUES	WED	THURS	FRI	SAT

2.ex.　①　②

3.ex. **MON**　①**TUES**　②**WED**

SUN	MON	TUES	WED	THURS	FRI	SAT

③　④　⑤

③ **FRI**　④ **SAT**　⑤ **SUN**

SUN	MON	TUES	WED	THURS	FRI	SAT

⑥　⑦　⑧

⑥ **THURS**　⑦ **FRI**　⑧ **SAT**

1. ex. おととい　ototoi

THE DAY BEFORE YESTERDAY	YESTERDAY	TODAY	
ex.	①	②	

2. ex. <u>おととい</u>は　<u>もくようびでした</u>。

<u>Ototoi</u> wa <u>moku-yōbi deshita</u>.

3. ex. A : <u>おととい</u>は　<u>すいようびでした</u>か。

B : いいえ、<u>すいようびではありませんでした</u>。

A : なんようび<u>でした</u>か。

B : <u>もくようびでした</u>。

A : <u>Ototoi</u> wa <u>sui-yōbi deshita</u> ka.

B : Iie, <u>sui-yōbi dewa arimasendeshita</u>.

A : Nan-yōbi <u>deshita</u> ka.

B : <u>Moku-yōbi deshita</u>.

SUN	MON	TUES	WED	THURS	FRI	SAT
				2.ex.	①	②
			3.ex. WED		① THURS	② FRI

SUN	MON	TUES	WED	THURS	FRI	SAT
③	④	⑤				

③ SAT　④ SUN　⑤ MON

SUN	MON	TUES	WED	THURS	FRI	SAT
	⑥	⑦	⑧			

⑥ SUN　⑦ MON　⑧ TUES

EXERCISES III

1. **ex.** にほんご　Nihon-go

2. **ex.** にほんごは　げつようびと　もくようびと　きんようびです。

Nihon-go wa getsu-yōbi to moku-yōbi to kin-yōbi desu.

3. **ex.** A : にほんごは　なんようびですか。

B : げつようびと　もくようびと　きんようびです。

A : Nihon-go wa nan-yōbi desu ka.

B : Getsu-yōbi to moku-yōbi to kin-yōbi desu.

	MON	TUES	WED	THURS	FRI	SAT
1	日本語 ex.	③ History	2πr²	日本語	English	⚽🏀
2	⚽🏀 ①	English ④	⑥ 🧪	2πr²	🧪	History
3	2πr² ②	🎨	⑤ 🎹	⑦ History	日本語	English

かようび	Tuesday	ka-yōbi
すいようび	Wednesday	sui-yōbi
あした	tomorrow	ashita
あさって	the day after tomorrow	asatte
なんようび	what day of the week	nan-yōbi
おととい	the day before yesterday	ototoi
えいご	English language	Ē-go
すうがく	mathematics	sūgaku
りか	science	rika
れきし	history	rekishi
おんがく	music	ongaku
たいいく	physical education	taiiku
びじゅつ	art	bijutsu

DAYS OF THE WEEK

にちようび	Sunday	nichi-yōbi
げつようび	Monday	getsu-yōbi
かようび	Tuesday	ka-yōbi
すいようび	Wednesday	sui-yōbi
もくようび	Thursday	moku-yōbi
きんようび	Friday	kin-yōbi
どようび	Saturday	do-yōbi

NUMBERS From 100 to 1000

100	ひゃく	hyaku
200	にひゃく	nihyaku
300	さんびゃく	sambyaku
400	よんひゃく	yonhyaku
500	ごひゃく	gohyaku
600	ろっぴゃく	roppyaku
700	ななひゃく	nanahyaku
800	はっぴゃく	happyaku
900	きゅうひゃく	kyūhyaku
1,000	せん	sen

MAIN TEXT

A WEEK

きょうは　すいようびです。　あしたは　もくようびです。

きのうは　かようびでした。

がっこうは　げつようびから　どようびまでです。

にちようびは　やすみです。

Kyō wa sui-yōbi desu.　Ashita wa moku-yōbi desu.
Kinō wa ka-yōbi deshita.
Gakkō wa getsu-yōbi kara do-yōbi made desu.
Nichi-yōbi wa yasumi desu.

VOCABULARY

やすみ	day off	yasumi

SHORT DIALOGUES

1

かとうくんの　おとうさん：にほんごの　べんきょうは　なんようび。

バードくん　　　　　　　：げつようびと　もくようびと　きんようびです。

Katō-kun no otōsan:　Nihon-go no benkyō wa nan-yōbi.
Bādo-kun:　　　　　　Getsu-yōbi to moku-yōbi to kin-yōbi desu.

2

たなかせんせい：きむらさん。

きむらさん　：はい。

たなかせんせい：バードくん。

バードくん　：はい。おそくなって、すみません。

Tanaka-sensē:　Kimura-san.
Kimura-san:　　Hai.
Tanaka-sensē:　Bādo-kun.
Bādo-kun:　　　Hai. Osoku natte, sumimasen.

3

みどりちゃん　：おかあさん、ごめんなさい。

Midori-chan:　　Okāsan, gomennasai.

VOCABULARY

はい	present (response in rollcall)	hai
おそくなって、すみません	I am sorry to be late	Osoku natte, sumimasen
すみません	I am sorry	sumimasen
みどりちゃん	(given name with diminutive title)	Midori-chan
〜ちゃん	-chan is used instead of -san when talking to young children or very close friends	-chan
おかあさん	mother (form of address)	okāsan
ごめんなさい	sorry (mostly used by small children or by women among close friends)	gomennasai

I. Match the days of the week as shown in the example.

ex.	Monday •	• すいようび	sui-yōbi
1.	Tuesday •	• もくようび	moku-yōbi
2.	Wednesday •	• げつようび	getsu-yōbi
3.	Thursday •	• きんようび	kin-yōbi
4.	Friday •	• どようび	do-yōbi
5.	Saturday •	• なんようび	nan-yōbi
6.	Sunday •	• にちようび	nichi-yōbi
7.	What day? •	• かようび	ka-yōbi

II. Fill in the blank with the appropriate day of the week.

1. きょうは げつようびです。

Kyō wa getsu-yōbi desu.

あしたは _____ です。

Ashita wa _____ desu.

きのうは _____ でした。

Kinō wa _____ deshita.

2. きょうは　きんようびです。

Kyō wa kin-yōbi desu.

あしたは ＿＿＿＿＿＿＿＿＿＿＿＿＿です。

Ashita wa ＿＿＿＿＿＿＿＿＿＿desu.

きのうは ＿＿＿＿＿＿＿＿＿＿＿＿＿でした。

Kinō wa ＿＿＿＿＿＿＿＿＿＿deshita.

III. Answer the following questions.

1. きょうは　すいようびです。　あしたは　もくようびですか。

Kyō wa sui-yōbi desu.　Ashita wa moku-yōbi desu ka.

→ ＿＿＿＿＿＿＿＿＿＿＿＿＿＿＿＿＿＿＿＿＿＿＿＿

＿＿＿＿＿＿＿＿＿＿＿＿＿＿＿＿＿＿＿＿＿＿＿＿＿＿＿

2. あしたは　にちようびです。　あさっては　かようびですか。

Ashita wa nichi-yōbi desu.　Asatte wa ka-yōbi desu ka.

→ ＿＿＿＿＿＿＿＿＿＿＿＿＿＿＿＿＿＿＿＿＿＿＿＿

＿＿＿＿＿＿＿＿＿＿＿＿＿＿＿＿＿＿＿＿＿＿＿＿＿＿＿

3. きのうは　どようびでした。　おとといは　きんようびでしたか。

Kinō wa do-yōbi deshita.　Ototoi wa kin-yōbi deshita ka.

→ ＿＿＿＿＿＿＿＿＿＿＿＿＿＿＿＿＿＿＿＿＿＿＿＿

＿＿＿＿＿＿＿＿＿＿＿＿＿＿＿＿＿＿＿＿＿＿＿＿＿＿＿

4. きのうは　げつようびでした。　きょうは　なんようびですか。

Kinō wa getsu-yōbi deshita.　Kyō wa nan-yōbi desu ka.

→ ＿＿＿＿＿＿＿＿＿＿＿＿＿＿＿＿＿＿＿＿＿＿＿＿

＿＿＿＿＿＿＿＿＿＿＿＿＿＿＿＿＿＿＿＿＿＿＿＿＿＿＿

IV. Answer the following questions.

1. がっこうは　なんようびから　なんようびまでですか。
Gakkō wa nan-yōbi kara nan-yōbi made desu ka.

→ _____

2. にほんごは　なんようびですか。
Nihon-go wa nan-yōbi desu ka.

→ _____

3. すうがくは　なんようびですか。
Sūgaku wa nan-yōbi desu ka.

→ _____

4. れきしは　なんようびですか。
Rekishi wa nan-yōbi desu ka.

→ _____

5. がっこうの　やすみは　なんようびですか。
Gakkō no yasumi wa nan-yōbi desu ka.

→ _____

MONTHS, DAYS OF THE MONTH

きのうは　あねの　たんじょうびでした。

KEY SENTENCES

1. ちちは　48さいです。

2. きょうは　6がつ　15にちです。

3. きのうは　あねの　たんじょうびでした。

1. Chichi wa yonjūhassai desu.
2. Kyō wa roku-gatsu jūgo-nichi desu.
3. Kinō wa ane no tanjōbi deshita.

☆ V O C A B U L A R Y ☆

ちち	my father	chichi
48さい	forty-eight years old	yonjūhassai
〜さい	-years old	-sai
6がつ　15にち	June 15	roku-gatsu jūgo-nichi
6がつ	June (lit. sixth month)	roku-gatsu
〜がつ	month	-gatsu
15にち	15th	jūgo-nichi
〜にち	day	-nichi
あね	my older sister	ane
たんじょうび	birthday	tanjōbi

EXERCISES I

1. **a. ex.** ちち
   chichi

   b. ex. おとうさん
   otōsan

| a. | **ex.** ちち chichi | ① |
| b. | **ex.** おとうさん otōsan | ① |

| ② | ③ | わたし watashi | ④ | ⑤ |
| ② | ③ | やまだくん Yamada-kun | ④ | ⑤ |

2. **ex.** バードくん： わたしは 13さいです。

   Bādo-kun:　　Watashi wa jūsan-sai desu.

3. **ex.** スミスさん： バードくんは なんさいですか。

   バードくん： 13さいです。

   Sumisu-san:　Bādo-kun wa nan-sai desu ka.
   Bādo-kun:　　Jūsan-sai desu.

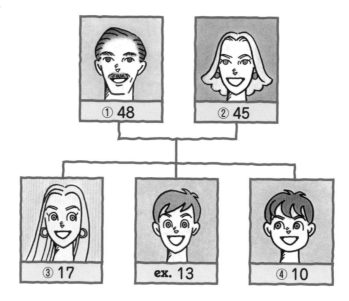

① 48　　　② 45

③ 17　　**ex.** 13　　④ 10

1. ex. いちがつ　ich-gatsu

JAN ex. | FEB ① | MAR ② | APR ③ | MAY ④ | JUN ⑤

JUL ⑥ | AUG ⑦ | SEPT ⑧ | OCT ⑨ | NOV ⑩ | DEC ⑪

2. a. ex 11にち　jūichi-nichi

SUN	MON	TUES	WED	THURS	FRI	SAT
						1
2	3	4 ex.	5 ①	6 ②	7	8 ③
9	10	⑪11	⑫12	⑬13	14	⑮15
④16	⑤17	⑥18	⑦19	20	⑧21	⑨22
⑩23	24	⑪25	⑫26	⑬27	⑭28	⑮29
⑯30	⑰31					

b. ex. みっか　mikka

3 ex. | 4 ① | 8 ② | 10 ③ | 2 ④ | 5 ⑤ | 20 ⑥

7 ⑦ | 9 ⑧ | 6 ⑨ | 1 ⑩ | 14 ⑪ | 24 ⑫

EXERCISES III

1. ex. バードくん： わたしの　たんじょうびは　1がつ　15にちです。
Bādo-kun:　　　Watashi no tanjōbi wa ichi-gatsu jūgo-nichi desu.

2. ex. A　　　：バードくんの　たんじょうびは　いつですか。

バードくん： 1がつ　15にちです。

A:　　　Bādo-kun no tanjōbi wa itsu desu ka.
Bādo-kun:　　Ichi-gatsu jūgo-nichi desu.

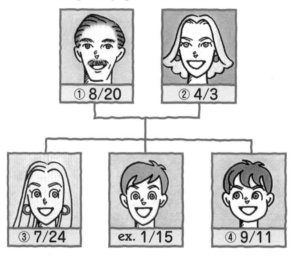

EXERCISES IV

ex. A：　おとといは　なんがつ　なんにちでしたか。

B：　4がつ　15にちでした。

A:　Ototoi wa nan-gatsu nan-nichi deshita ka.
B:　Shi-gatsu jūgo-nichi deshita.

APR

SUN	MON	TUES	WED	THURS	FRI	SAT
					1	2
3	4	5	6	7	8	9
10	11	12	13	14	15 ex.	16 ①
17 ②	18 ③	19 ④	20	21	22	23
24	25	26	27	28	29	30

はは	my mother	haha
あに	my older brother	ani
おとうと	my younger brother	otōto
いもうと	my younger sister	imōto
おかあさん	(someone else's) mother	okāsan
おにいさん	(someone else's) older brother	oniisan
おねえさん	(someone else's) older sister	onēsan
おとうとさん	(someone else's) younger brother	otōto-san
いもうとさん	(someone else's) younger sister	imōto-san
なんさい	how old	nan-sai
いつ	when	itsu
なんがつ	which month	nan-gatsu
なんにち	which day of the month	nan-nichi

MONTHS

いちがつ	January	ichi-gatsu	しちがつ	July	shichi-gatsu
にがつ	February	ni-gatsu	はちがつ	August	hachi-gatsu
さんがつ	March	san-gatsu	くがつ	September	ku-gatsu
しがつ	April	shi-gatsu	じゅうがつ	October	jū-gatsu
ごがつ	May	go-gatsu	じゅういちがつ	November	jūichi-gatsu
ろくがつ	June	roku-gatsu	じゅうにがつ	December	jūni-gatsu

DAYS OF THE MONTH

ついたち	1st	tsuitachi	じゅうしちにち	17th	jūshichi-nichi
ふつか	2nd	futsuka	じゅうはちにち	18th	jūhachi-nichi
みっか	3rd	mikka	じゅうくにち	19th	jūku-nichi
よっか	4th	yokka	はつか	20th	hatsuka
いつか	5th	itsuka	にじゅういちにち	21st	nijūichi-nichi
むいか	6th	muika	にじゅうににち	22nd	nijūni-nichi
なのか	7th	nanoka	にじゅうさんにち	23rd	nijūsan-nichi
ようか	8th	yōka	にじゅうよっか	24th	nijūyokka
ここのか	9th	kokonoka	にじゅうごにち	25th	nijūgo-nichi
とおか	10th	tōka	にじゅうろくにち	26th	nijūroku-nichi
じゅういちにち	11th	jūichi-nichi	にじゅうしちにち	27th	nijūshichi-nichi
じゅうににち	12th	jūni-nichi	にじゅうはちにち	28th	nijūhachi-nichi
じゅうさんにち	13th	jūsan-nichi	にじゅうくにち	29th	nijūku-nichi
じゅうよっか	14th	jūyokka	さんじゅうにち	30th	sanjū-nichi
じゅうごにち	15th	jūgo-nichi	さんじゅういちにち	31st	sanjūichi-nichi
じゅうろくにち	16th	jūroku-nichi			

MAIN DIALOGUE

Yesterday was Bādo-kun's older sister's birthday.

バードくん　　　：　きのうは　あねの　たんじょうびでした。

たなかせんせい：　おねえさんは　なんさいですか。

バードくん　　　：　17さいです。

　　　　　　　　　　せんせいの　たんじょうびは　いつですか。

たなかせんせい：　7がつ　15にちです。

☺ きのうは　バードくんの　おねえさんの　たんじょうびでした。

　　おねえさんは　17さいです。

Bādo-kun:　　　　　Kinō wa ane no tanjōbi deshita.
Tanaka-sensē:　　 Onēsan wa nan-sai desu ka.
Bādo-kun:　　　　　Jūnana-sai desu.　Sensē no tanjōbi wa itsu desu ka.
Tanaka-sensē:　　 Shichi-gatsu jūgo-nichi desu.

☺ Kinō wa Bādo-kun no onēsan no tanjōbi deshita.
　 Onēsan wa jūnana-sai desu.

SHORT DIALOGUES

1

バードくん　　　：　なつやすみは　なんがつ。

やまもとくん　：　7がつと　8がつ。

バードくん　　　：　7がつ　なんにちから。

やまもとくん　：　25にちから。

Bādo-kun:　　　　　　Natsu-yasumi wa nan-gatsu.
Yamamoto-kun:　　　Shichi-gatsu to hachi-gatsu.
Bādo-kun:　　　　　　Shichi-gatsu nan-nichi kara.
Yamamoto-kun:　　　Nijūgo-nichi kara.

2

やまもとくんの　おかあさん　：　みどりちゃんは　なんさい。

みどりちゃん　　　　　　　　　：　5さいです。

Yamamoto-kun no okāsan:　　Midori-chan wa nan-sai?
Midori-chan:　　　　　　　　　5-sai desu.

3

かとうくんの　おかあさん　：　あぶない。　だいじょうぶ？

バードくん　　　　　　　　　：　はい、だいじょうぶです。

Katō-kun no okāsan:　　Abunai. Daijōbu?
Bādo-kun:　　　　　　　　Hai, daijōbu desu.

⋆ V O C A B U L A R Y ⋆

なつやすみ	summer vacation	natsu-yasumi
なつ	summer	natsu
やすみ	vacation, holiday	yasumi
あぶない	be careful (-i adj.)(See NOTE)	abunai
だいじょうぶ（な）	OK, all right (-na adj.)	daijōbu(na)

 There are two types of adjective in Japanese: -i and -na adjectives. You will learn how to use adjectives in Lessons 8 and 9.

SUMMARY TABLE •

で　す

Present Form		Past Form	
aff.	**neg.**	**aff.**	**neg.**
です desu	ではありません dewa arimasen	でした deshita	ではありませんでした dewa arimasendeshita

In everyday speech ja arimasen and ja arimasendeshita are often used instead of dewa arimasen and dewa arimasendeshita. Ja is considered more informal than dewa.

T A S K ❸

ともだちの　かぞく*¹

Talk about your family with a friend. Then listen to your friend talk about their family and draw their family tree.

ex.

スミスさん　：　わたしの　かぞくは　ちちと　ははと　おとうとです。

おとうとは　ふたり*² です。

Sumisu-san:　　Watashi no kazoku wa chichi to haha to otōto desu.
　　　　　　　　Otōto wa futari desu.

*¹ かぞく	family	kazoku
*² ひとり	one person	hitori
ふたり	two people	futari
さんにん	three people	san-nin
〜にん	counter for people	-nin

Find out everyone's age and birthday and add that information to the family tree.

ex.

バードくん　：　おとうとさんは　なんさいですか。

スミスさん　：　10さいと　8さいです。

バードくん　：　10さいの　おとうとさんの　たんじょうびは　いつですか。

スミスさん　：　4がつ　いつかです。

Bādo-kun:　　　Otōto-san wa nan-sai desu ka.
Sumisu-san:　　Jussai to hassai desu.
Bādo-kun:　　　Jussai no otōto-san no tanjōbi wa itsu desu ka.
Sumisu-san:　　Shi-gatsu itsuka desu.

ex.

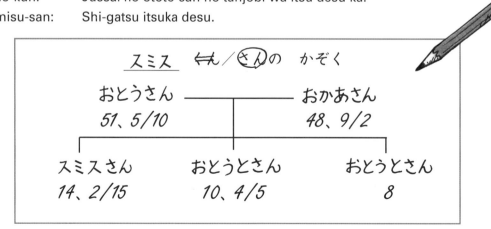

LET'S TRY!

_____ くん／さんの　かぞく

QUIZ

I. Write each month in Hiragana.

ex.	1 (　いち　) がつ	**6.**	7 (　　　　) がつ
1.	2 (　　　　) がつ	**7.**	8 (　　　　) がつ
2.	3 (　　　　) がつ	**8.**	9 (　　　　) がつ
3.	4 (　　　　) がつ	**9.**	10 (　　　　) がつ
4.	5 (　　　　) がつ	**10.**	11 (　　　　) がつ
5.	6 (　　　　) がつ	**11.**	12 (　　　　) がつ

II. Write the appropriate month and date in Hiragana.

1. きょうは　しがつ　ここのかです。
Kyō wa shi-gatsu kokonoka desu.

→あしたは ______________________ です。

Ashita wa ______________________ desu.

→きのうは ______________________ でした。

Kinō wa ______________________ deshita.

2. きょうは　しちがつ　ふつかです。

Kyō wa shichi-gatsu futsuka desu.

→あしたは _____ です。

Ashita wa _____ desu.

→きのうは _____ でした。

Kinō wa _____ deshita.

3. きょうは　くがつ　いつかです。

Kyō wa ku-gatsu itsuka desu.

→あしたは _____ です。

Ashita wa _____ desu.

→きのうは _____ でした。

Kinō wa _____ deshita.

III. Complete the questions so that they fit the answers.

1. A：いま　（ _____ ）ですか。

Ima (_____) desu ka.

B：4がつです。

Shi-gatsu desu.

2. A：きょうは　（ _____ ）ですか。

Kyō wa (_____) desu ka.

B：10かです。

Tōka desu.

QUIZ

3. A : (   ) ですか。

     (   ) desu ka.

    B : 10さいです。

     Jussai desu.

4. A : いま　(   ) ですか。

     Ima (   ) desu ka.

    B : 10じです。

     Jū-ji desu.

5. A : きょうは　(   ) ですか。

     Kyō wa (   ) desu ka.

    B : かようびです。

     Ka-yōbi desu.

IV. Answer the following questions.

1. なんさいですか。

Nan-sai desu ka.

→ _____

2. たんじょうびは　いつですか。

Tanjōbi wa itsu desu ka.

→ _____

3. せんせいの　たんじょうびは　なんがつ　なんにちですか。

Sensē no tanjōbi wa nan-gatsu nan-nichi desu ka.

→ _____

4. なつやすみは　いつから　いつまでですか。

Natsu-yasumi wa itsu kara itsu made desu ka.

→ _____

それは　いくらですか。

KEY SENTENCES

1. これは　とけいです。　それも　とけいです。

2. あれは　500えんです。

3. これを　ください。　あれも　ください。

1. Kore wa tokē desu. Sore mo tokē desu.
2. Are wa gohyaku-en desu.
3. Kore o kudasai. Are mo kudasai.

V O C A B U L A R Y

それ	that, that one (See SUMMARY TABLE on p.81)	sore
も	too, also (particle)	mo
あれ	that, that one (See SUMMARY TABLE on p.81)	are
500えん	500 yen	gohyaku-en
〜えん	yen (¥)	-en
を	(object marker, particle)	o
ください	Please give me.	kudasai

EXERCISES I

1. ex. これ

2. ex. これは　ノートです。

3. ex. バードくん　　：　これは　ノートですか。

たなかせんせい：　はい、ノートです。

4. ex. バードくん　　　： これは　ほんですか。

たなかせんせい： いいえ、ほんではありません。

バードくん　　　： なんですか。

たなかせんせい： ノートです。

ex.

①

②

EXERCISES II

1. ex. これを　ください。

①

②

2. a. ex. みず

　　b. ex. えんぴつ

3. a. ex. みずを　ください。

　　b.ex. えんぴつを　ください。

a

b

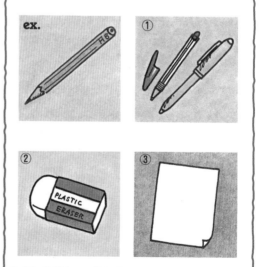

JAPAN NEWS

There is only one unit of currency in Japan and that is yen. Rather than have two units, e.g. dollars and cents, all calculations are in yen only. Since one yen is roughly equivalent to one cent, large numbers are needed when talking about prices.

The yen mark is written ¥, which is Y with two lines crossed through horizontally.

The denominations of Japanese currency are as follows. The coins are ¥1, ¥5, ¥10, ¥50, ¥100, and ¥500. The bills are ¥1,000, ¥5,000, and ¥10,000.

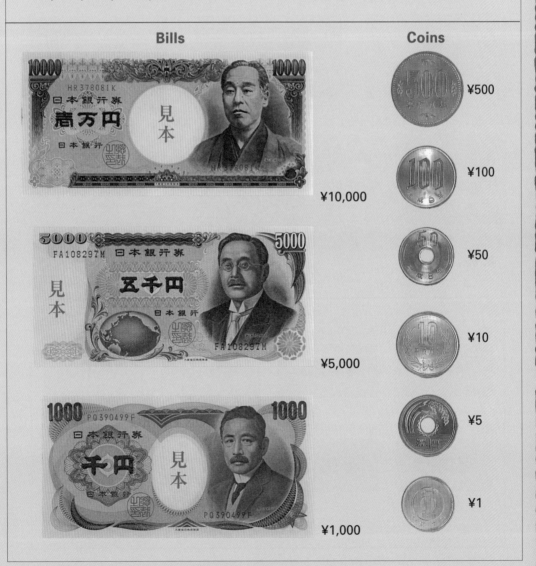

Bills	Coins
¥10,000	¥500
¥5,000	¥100
¥1,000	¥50
	¥10
	¥5
	¥1

EXERCISES III

1. a. ex. 100えん

ex.

①

②

③

④

⑤

⑥

⑦

⑧

⑨

b. ex. 260えん

ex.	①	②	③
¥260	¥420	¥540	¥680

④	⑤	⑥	⑦
¥890	¥927	¥1,600	¥1,730

2. ex. A： トマトは　いくらですか。

B： 350えんです。

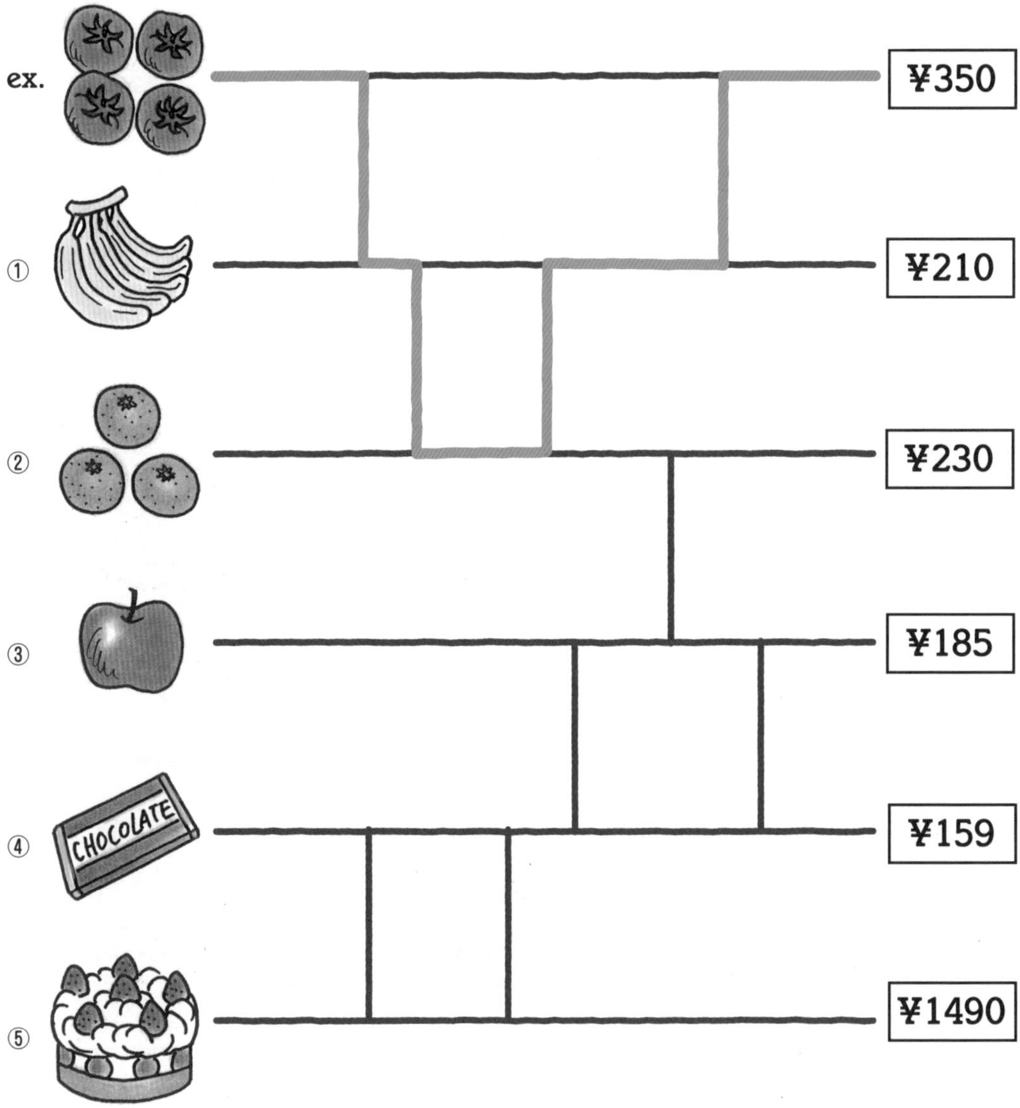

ex. ¥350

① ¥210

② ¥230

③ ¥185

④ ¥159

⑤ ¥1490

Find out how to play the "Amida-Kuji Game" on page 155.

EXERCISES Ⅳ

ex. これは　えんぴつです。
これも　えんぴつです。
これは　けしゴムです。

ex.

①

②

✪ VOCABULARY ✪

ちず	map	chizu
みず	water	mizu
おちゃ	green tea, tea in general	o-cha
お〜	(prefix) (See NOTE)	o-
レシート	receipt	reshiito
ペン	pen	pen
けしゴム	eraser	keshigomu
かみ	paper	kami
いくら	how much	ikura

 The prefix o- is traditionally added to certain words to make them sound nicer. Other examples include o-bentō (box lunch) and o-hashi (chopsticks) in this lesson (Short Dialogues) and o-sake (saké) in Lesson 10.

MAIN DIALOGUE

Bādo-kun goes shopping at the stationery store.
He doesn't know how to say scissors in Japanese.

みせの　ひと：いらっしゃいませ。

バードくん　　：あれを　みせてください。

みせの　ひと：はい、どうぞ。

バードくん　　：これは　いくらですか。

みせの　ひと：500えんです。

バードくん　　：それは　いくらですか。

みせの　ひと：これも　500えんです。

バードくん　　：じゃあ、これを　ください。

VOCABULARY

みせの　ひと	store clerk	mise no hito
みせ	store, shop	mise
ひと	person	hito
いらっしゃいませ	Come in/Welcome	irasshaimase
	(greeting to customers in stores/restaurants)	
みせてください	Please show me.	misete kudasai
どうぞ	Here you are.	dōzo
じゃあ	Well then (See NOTE)	jā

 Jā is used to show that you have made your mind up about something. It usually comes at the beginning of the sentence that expresses this decision. In this dialogue, Mike Bird uses it to let the sales clerk know that he has made up his mind.

SHORT DIALOGUES

1

バードくん ：おべんとうを　ください。

かとうくんの　おかあさん：はい、どうぞ。

バードくん ：おはしも　ください。

2

バードくん　：あれは　いくらですか。

みせの　ひと：どれですか。

バードくん　：あれです。

JAPAN NEWS

An *o-bentō* is a special kind of Japanese packed lunch. Instead of sandwiches, rolls, or bagels, this lunch is often based on rice, with a meat or fish side dish and cooked or raw vegetables. School kids often compete to have the most delicious-looking *o-bentō*. Girls like to swap parts of their lunch with their friends. In its simplest form, an *ume-boshi* or pickled plum is put in the middle of the white rice, creating a "*Hinomaru bentō*." (*Hinomaru* is the offical name of the Japanese national flag.) Best enjoyed with chopsticks and a cup of green tea.

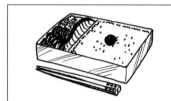

3

やまもとくん：バードくんの
　　　　　　　じてんしゃは　どれ。

バードくん　：それ。

VOCABULARY

おべんとう	box lunch	o-bentō
おはし	chopsticks	o-hashi
どれ	which one (See SUMMARY TABLE on p.81)	dore
じてんしゃ	bicycle	jitensha

TASK 4

ノートと えんぴつと けしゴムを ください。

B goes shopping at a stationery store where A is the sales clerk. B chooses three items and asks A to calculate the total price. A adds up the prices given in the list and tells B the total.

ex.

A： いらっしゃいませ。

B： <u>ノートと えんぴつと けしゴムを</u> ください。

A： <u>ノートと えんぴつと けしゴム</u>ですね。

B： ぜんぶで*¹ いくらですか。

A： ちょっと まってください。
　　 ぜんぶで <u>360えん</u>です。

*¹ぜんぶで in total zembu de

ex.

✔	ノート	¥150
☐	かみ	¥20
✔	えんぴつ	¥80
✔	けしゴム	¥130
☐	ペン	¥350
☐	そろばん	¥1,500
☐	かばん	¥1,800
	TOTAL	¥360

LET'S TRY!

☐	ノート	¥150
☐	かみ	¥20
☐	えんぴつ	¥80
☐	けしゴム	¥130
☐	ペン	¥350
☐	そろばん	¥1,500
☐	かばん	¥1,800
	TOTAL	¥

C C

I. Put the appropriate particles in the parentheses.

1. あれ（　　　　）みせてください。

2. これ（　　　　）いくらですか。

3. これ（　　　　）ください。

4. これ（　　　　）500えんです。　それ（　　　　）500えんです。

C C

II. Complete the questions so that they fit the answers.

1. A：それは（　　　　　　　）ですか。

　　B：これですか。　けしゴムです。

2. A：これは　（　　　　　　　）ですか。

　　B：それは　300えんです。

3. A：（　　　　　　　）は　なんですか。

　　B：あれは　とけいです。

III. Answer the following questions using the most appropriate word from the list given below.

それ・１７さい・１がつ　１５にち・５０えん

1. これは　いくらですか。

   → _____

2. バードくんの　おねえさんは　なんさいですか。

   → _____

3. けんくんの　ほんは　どれですか。

   → _____

4. バードくんの　たんじょうびは　いつですか。

   → _____

IV. Match the number to the correct word as shown in the example.

ex. さんびゃく ·   **400**

1. にひゃく   ·   **800**

2. はっぴゃく ·   **100**

3. ろっぴゃく ·   **500**

4. よんひゃく ·   **200**

5. ひゃく   ·   **600**

6. せん   ·   **1,000**

7. ごひゃく   ·   **300**

8. きゅうひゃく ·   **900**

9. ななひゃく ·   **700**

その りんごを みっつ ください。

KEY SENTENCES

1. この ペンは 120えんです。

2. これは にほんの とけいです。

3. この えんぴつは 1ぽん 50えんです。

4. その りんごを みっつ ください。

1. Kono pen wa hyaku nijū-en desu.
2. Kore wa Nihon no tokē desu.
3. Kono empitsu wa ippon gojū-en desu.
4. Sono ringo o mittsu kudasai.

V O C A B U L A R Y

この	this (See SUMMARY TABLE on p.81)	kono
にほんの	Japanese (made in Japan)	Nihon no
1ぽん	1	ippon
〜ほん、ぼん、ぽん	(counter for long slender objects such as pencils, bottles, and their contents etc.) (See NOTE)	-hon, -bon, -pon
その	that (See SUMMARY TABLE on p.81)	sono
みっつ	3 (things) (See NOTE)	mittsu

 Two numerical systems are used in Japanese: the **hitotsu, futatsu, mittsu** system and the abstract **ichi, ni, san** system. Compare both in the charts on p.86.

EXERCISES I

1. ex. シャツ

① ② ③ ④ ⑤ ⑥

2. ex. この　りんご

3. ex. この　りんごを　ください。

ex.

① ②

4. ex. バードくん　：この　みかんは　いくらですか。

みせの　ひと：　20えんです。

SUMMARY TABLE •

こ-そ-あ-ど

	こ-words	そ-words	あ-words	ど-words
thing	これ this	それ that	あれ that over there	どれ which
demonstrative	この　ほん this book	その　ほん that book	あの　ほん that book over there	どの　ほん which book

EXERCISES II

1. ex. ドイツ

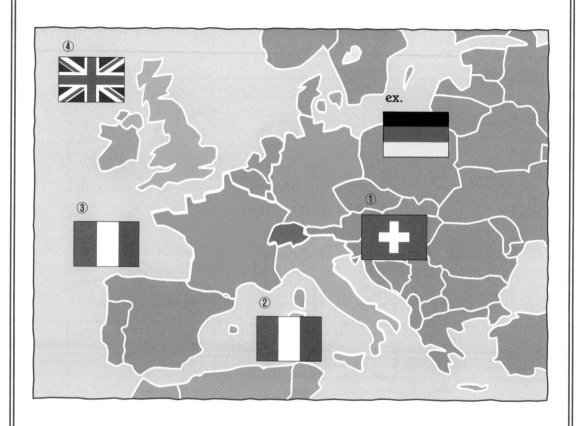

2. ex. ドイツの　えんぴつ

3. ex. バードくん　　　：　それは　どこの　とけいですか。

たなかせんせい：　スイスの　とけいです。

4. ex. バードくん　　：　この　ドイツの　えんぴつは　いくらですか。

みせの　ひと：　120えんです。

EXERCISES III

1. a. ex. いちまい

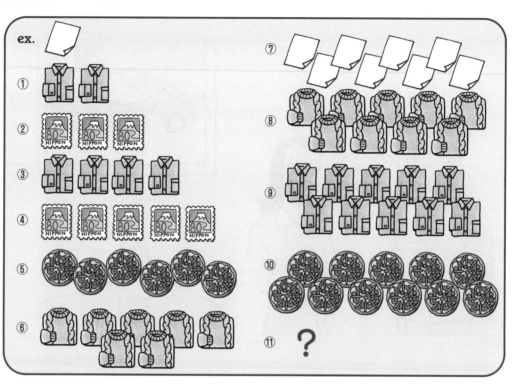

b. ex. いっぽん

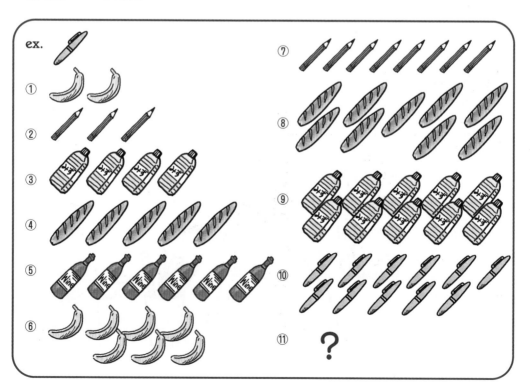

c. ex. ひとつ

2. a. ex. この　かみは　1まい　50えんです。

ex. ¥50
① ¥60
② ¥3,000
③ ¥500

b. ex. この　えんぴつは　1ぽん　70えんです。

ex. ¥70
① ¥100
② ¥1,800
③ ¥220

c. ex. この　けしゴムは　ひとつ　200えんです。

ex.

¥200

①

¥150

②

¥30

③

¥140

3. ex. この　かみを　2まい　ください。

COUNTING: general objects

ひとつ	1	hitotsu
ふたつ	2	futatsu
みっつ	3	mittsu
よっつ	4	yottsu
いつつ	5	itsutsu
むっつ	6	muttsu
ななつ	7	nanatsu
やっつ	8	yattsu
ここのつ	9	kokonotsu
とお	10	tō

COUNTING: long slender objects

1ぽん（いっぽん）	ippon
2ほん（にほん）	ni-hon
3ぽん（さんぼん）	san-bon
4ほん（よんほん）	yon-hon
5ほん（ごほん）	go-hon
6ぽん（ろっぽん）	roppon
7ほん（ななほん）	nana-hon
8ぽん（はっぽん）	happon
9ほん（きゅうほん）	kyū-hon
10ぽん（じゅっぽん）	juppon

シャツ	shirt	shatsu
セーター	sweater	sētā
パン	bread	pan
ピザ	pizza	piza
アイスクリーム	ice cream	aisukuriimu
ワイン	wine	wain
あの	that (over there) (See SUMMARY TABLE on p.81)	ano
ドイツ	Germany	Doitsu
イタリア	Italy	Itaria
フランス	France	Furansu
スイス	Switzerland	Suisu
ドイツの	German	Doitsu no
どこの	of which country	doko no
1まい	1	ichi-mai
～まい	(counter for thin, flat objects such as paper, records, etc.)	-mai
なんまい	how many	nan-mai
なんぼん	how many	nan-bon
いくつ	how many	ikutsu

NUMBERS From 1,000 to 100,000

1,000	せん	sen
2,000	にせん	nisen
3,000	さんぜん	sanzen
4,000	よんせん	yonsen
5,000	ごせん	gosen
6,000	ろくせん	rokusen
7,000	ななせん	nanasen
8,000	はっせん	hassen
9,000	きゅうせん	kyūsen
10,000	いちまん	ichi-man
100,000	じゅうまん	jū-man

MAIN DIALOGUE

Bādo-kun goes back to the stationery shop.

バードくん　　：　すみません、その　ペンは　いくらですか。

みせの　ひと：　どれですか。

バードくん　　：　その　ペンです。

みせの　ひと：　これですか。　1,200えんです。　どうぞ。

バードくん　　：　これを　ください。

　　　　　　　　　それから　えんぴつを　3ぼん　ください。

みせの　ひと：　ぜんぶで　1,350えんです。

☺　ペンは　1,200えんです。　えんぴつは　1ぽん　50えんです。

VOCABULARY

それから	and	sorekara

SHORT DIALOGUES

1

バードくん	： かぞくの しゃしんです。
	ちちです。 ははです。 あねです。
かとうくんの おかあさん	： この おんなの ひとは どなたですか。
バードくん	： ははの ともだちです。
かとうくんの おかあさん	： この おとこの こは？
バードくん	： おとうとです。

2

きむらさん	： これは バードくんの とけい？
バードくん	： うん。
きむらさん	： どこの。
バードくん	： にほんの。

3

バードくん	： えんぴつを 10ぽん ください。
みせの ひと	： どの えんぴつですか。
バードくん	： その ドイツの えんぴつです。
みせの ひと	： これですね。 1ぽん 120えんです。
バードくん	： じゃあ、5ほん ください。

VOCABULARY

しゃしん	photograph	shashin
おんなの ひと	woman	onna no hito
おんな	woman, female	onna
どなた	who (polite word for **dare**)	donata
おとこの こ	boy	otoko no ko
おとこ	man, male	otoko
こ	child	ko
どの	which (See SUMMARY TABLE on p.81)	dono

TASK 5

みずを　3ぼん　ください。

A goes shopping at three stores where B is the sales clerk. A asks for a specific number of a specific product, e.g. 3 bottles of mineral water, and B then circles the correct number of the correct product on the illustration.

ex.

A : すみません、みずを　3ぼん　ください。

B : どの　みずですか。

A : その　みずです。

B : はい。3ぼんですね。

Let's try!

1.

2.

【CC】

I. Write the appropriate particles in the parentheses.
(If a particle is not required, put an X in the parentheses.)

1. これ（　　　）わたし（　　　）ペンです。

2. この（　　　）けしゴム（　　　）わたし（　　　）です。

3. それ（　　　）にほん（　　　）くるま（　　　）です。

4. その（　　　）りんご（　　　）ひとつ（　　　）ください。

5. あの（　　　）えんぴつ（　　　）1ぽん（　　　）50えんです。

【CC】

II. Write down how to count things in Hiragana as shown in the example.

ex.  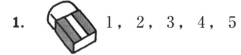 1, 2, 3

→いっぽん、にほん、さんぼん

1. 1, 2, 3, 4, 5

→

2. 1, 2, 3

→

3.   1, 2, 3, 4, 5, 6

→

III. Circle the correct word from the options given in parentheses.

1. A：（これ・この）　セーターは　だれのですか。

　　 B：（それ・その）　は　わたしのです。

2. A：（あれ・あの）　を　みせてください。

　　 B：（どれ・どの）　ですか。

3. A：（これ・この）　は　100えんです。

　　 B：じゃあ、（それ・その）　ペンを　1ぽん　ください。

IV. Put the following words in order and make a statement.

1. その・みっつ・みかんを・ください

　　 →
　　 _____

2. あの・ですか・いくら・シャツは

　　 →
　　 _____

3. とけい・これは・スイスの・です

　　 →
　　 _____

4. です・かみは・20えん・この・1まい

　　 →
　　 _____

V. Match the number to the correct word as shown in the example.

ex. にせん		·	**5,000**
1. ろくせん	·	·	**8,000**
2. きゅうせん	·	·	**3,000**
3. ななせん	·	·	**6,000**
4. よんせん	·	·	**4,000**
5. じゅうまん	·	·	**1,000**
6. せん	·	·	**10,000**
7. はっせん	·	·	**9,000**
8. いちまん	·	·	**2,000**
9. ごせん	·	·	**7,000**
10. さんぜん	·	·	**100,000**

おおきい　ポテトを　ください。

KEY SENTENCES

1. あかい　ペンを　1ぽん　ください。
2. ポテトを　ひとつと　コーラを　ふたつ　ください。
3. おおきい　ポテトを　ひとつと　ちいさい　コーラを
　　ふたつ　ください。

1. Akai pen o ippon kudasai.
2. Poteto o hitotsu to kōra o futatsu kudasai.
3. Ōkii poteto o hitotsu to chiisai kōra o futatsu kudasai.

☆ V O C A B U L A R Y ☆

あかい	red (-i adj.)	akai
ポテト	fried potato, potato	poteto
コーラ	coke	kōra
おおきい	large, big (-i adj.)	ōkii
ちいさい	small (-i adj.)	chiisai

EXERCISES I

1. ex. ハンバーガー

 ①　 ②　 ③　 ④　 ⑤　 ⑥

2. ex. おおきい　りんご
　　　　ちいさい　りんご

3. ex. おおきい　りんごを　ください。
　　　　ちいさい　りんごを　ください。

ex.

 ①　 ②　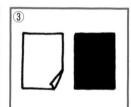 ③　 ④

4. ex. おおきい　かみを　3まい　ください。

ex.

 ①　 ②　 ③

 ④　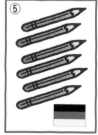 ⑤　 ⑥　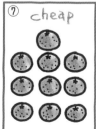 ⑦　 ⑧

1. ex. りんごと　みかんを　ください。

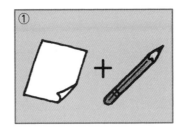

2. ex. りんごを　ひとつと　みかんを　ふたつ　ください。

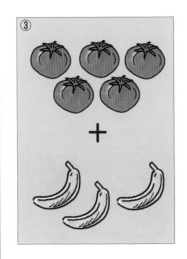

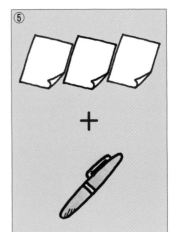

EXERCISES III

1. ex. おおきい　ポテトと　ちいさい　ポテトを　ください。

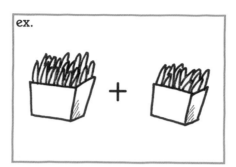

expensive　cheap

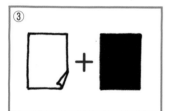

¥100-　¥120-
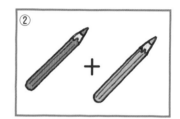

2. ex. あかい　かみを　5まいと　あおい　かみを　8まい　ください。

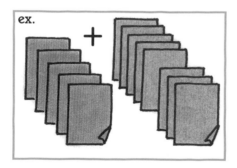

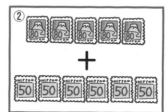

VOCABULARY

ハンバーガー	hamburger	hambāgā
サラダ	salad	sarada
ジュース	juice	jūsu
ミルク	milk	miruku
コーヒー	coffee	kōhii
たかい	expensive (i-adj.)	takai
やすい	cheap (i-adj.)	yasui
あおい	blue (i-adj.)	aoi
しろい	white (i-adj.)	shiroi
くろい	black (i-adj.)	kuroi

MAIN DIALOGUE

Bādo-kun and Yamamoto-kun go to a hamburger shop.

みせの　ひと：いらっしゃいませ。

バードくん　：ハンバーガーを　ふたつ　ください。

みせの　ひと：はい、ハンバーガーを　ふたつですね。

バードくん　：それから　おおきい　ポテトを　ひとつと

　　　　　　　ちいさい　コーラを　ふたつ　ください。

みせの　ひと：はい、しょうしょう　おまちください。

VOCABULARY

しょうしょう	a moment (more formal than chotto)	shōshō
おまちください	Please wait. (politer than matte kudasai)	o-machi kudasai
まちます（まつ）	wait	machimasu (matsu)

SHORT DIALOGUES

1

バードくん　　　　：メニューを　みせてください。

みせの　ひと　　　：はい、どうぞ。

バードくん　　　　：コーヒーを　ふたつと　ケーキを　ひとつ　ください。

2

きむらさん　　　　：なんの　ざっし。

バードくん　　　　：くるまの　ざっし。

きむらさん　　　　：みせて。

3

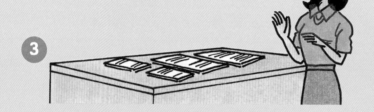

バードくん　　　　：すみません、プリントを　もう　1まい　ください。

たなかせんせい：どの　プリント。

バードくん　　　　：その　ちいさい　プリントです。

たなかせんせい：あ、これですね。　はい、どうぞ。

VOCABULARY

メニュー	menu	menyū
なんの	what kind of	nan no
プリント	print-out	purinto
もう	more	mō
あ	ah	a

ちいさい　ハンバーガーを　ふたつと
おおきい　ポテトを　ひとつ　ください。

B goes to eat at a fast food store where A is a sales clerk. B orders from the menu provided and A tells B how much it comes to in total. B pays with a bill and A gives B the change.

ex.

A ： いらっしゃいませ。

B ： <u>ちいさい　ハンバーガーを　ふたつと
おおきい　ポテトを　ひとつ</u>　ください。

A ： はい、しょうしょう　おまちください。　ぜんぶで　<u>480えん</u>です。

B ： <u>1000えん</u>で　おねがいします[*1]。

A ： <u>520えん</u>の　おつりです[*2]。　ありがとうございました。

       [*1] ～で　おねがいします　　Please take it out of ¥～. – de o-negai shimasu
       [*2] ～の　おつりです　　　　Here is your change, ¥～. – no o-tsuri desu

ex.

☐ ハンバーガー	(Large)	¥ 300 ×		=	
☑	(Small)	¥ 150 ×	*2*	=	*300*
☑ ポテト	(L)	¥ 180 ×	*1*	=	*180*

TOTAL	¥*480*
CASH	¥*1000*
CHANGE	¥*520*

Let's try!

☐ ハンバーガー	(L)	¥ 300 ×	=	
☐	(S)	¥ 150 ×	=	
☐ ポテト	(L)	¥ 180 ×	=	
☐	(S)	¥ 120 ×	=	
☐ コーラ	(L)	¥ 160 ×	=	
☐	(S)	¥ 130 ×	=	
☐ ジュース	(L)	¥ 170 ×	=	
☐	(S)	¥ 140 ×	=	
☐ ミルク	(L)	¥ 230 ×	=	
☐	(S)	¥ 190 ×	=	
☐ コーヒー		¥ 150 ×	=	
☐ サラダ		¥ 200 ×	=	
☐ アイスクリーム		¥ 110 ×	=	

TOTAL	¥
CASH	¥
CHANGE	¥

I. Write the appropriate particles in the parentheses.

(If a particle is not required, put an ✕ in the parentheses.)

1. コーヒー（　　　）ふたつ（　　　）ください。

2. 80えん（　　　）きって（　　　）5まい（　　　）ください。

3. ハンバーガー（　　　）ポテト（　　　）ください。

4. サラダ（　　　）ひとつ（　　　）ミルク（　　　）ふたつ
（　　　）ください。

II. Complete the questions so that they fit the answers.

1. A：これは（　　　　　　）の　きってですか。

　　B：カナダの　きってです。

2. A：それは（　　　　　　）の　かばんですか。

　　B：みどりちゃんのです。

3. A：それは（　　　　　　）の　ほんですか。

　　B：そろばんの　ほんです。

4. A：ちいさい　みかんを　ください。

　　B：（　　　　　　）ですか。

　　A：いつつ　ください。

III. Make sentences as shown in the example.

ex. かみ・ください・2 まい・あかい

→ あかい　かみを　2 まい　ください。
_____

1. えんぴつ・20 えん・1 ぽん・ください

→
_____

2. ひとつ・パン・120 えんです・ドイツ

→
_____

3. みかん・30 えんです・ちいさい・ひとつ

→
_____

4. ください・バナナ・よっつ・3 ぼん・トマト

→
_____

5. 1 ぽん・ピザ・ください・3 まい・ワイン

→
_____

IV. Make sentences as shown in the example.

ex.

→あおい　えんぴつを　3ぼんと　あかい　かみを　2まい　ください。

1.

→ _____

2.

→ _____

3.

¥20

→ _____

A FAMOUS TEMPLE

これは ゆうめいな おてらです。

KEY SENTENCES

1. さくらは きれいな はなです。
2. きょうとは どんな まちですか。

1. Sakura wa kirēna hana desu.
2. Kyōto wa donna machi desu ka.

VOCABULARY

さくら	cherry blossoms	sakura
きれいな	pretty, beautiful, clean (-na adj.)	kirēna
はな	flower	hana
きょうと	Kyoto (city and prefecture)	Kyōto
どんな	what kind of	donna
まち	town, city	machi

EXERCISES 〈 I 〉

1. a. ex. はな

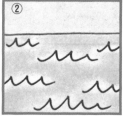
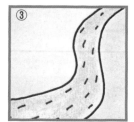

b. ex. こども

2. a. ex. きれいな　はな

　① famous
　② beautiful
　③ famous
　④ quiet

⑤ quiet

⑥ beautiful place

b. ex. げんきな　こども

ex. healthy

① healthy

② healthy

③ kind

④ kind

3. ex. さくらは　きれいな　はなです。

ex.  ....

①  ....

②  ....

③  ....

④  ....

⑤  ....

EXERCISES II

ex.　バードくん　　：さくらは　どんな　はなですか。

　　　たなかせんせい：きれいな　はなです。

やま	mountain	yama
うみ	sea, ocean	umi
かわ	river	kawa
こうえん	park	kōen
ところ	place	tokoro
こども	child	kodomo
おんなの　こ	girl	onna no ko
おとこの　ひと	man	otoko no hito
ゆうめいな	famous (-na adj.)	yumēna
しずかな	quiet (-na adj.)	shizukana
げんきな	healthy (not used for things), cheerful (-na adj.)	genkina
しんせつな	kind (-na adj.)	shinsetsuna
ふじさん	Mt. Fuji (the highest mountain in Japan)	fuji-san

JAPAN NEWS

A Temple in Kyoto

Kyoto is an old and famous city located in the Kansai region, which is about 300 miles due west of the capital Tokyo. In fact until the end of the nineteenth century, Kyoto was the capital of Japan and home to its emperor and imperial family.

Kyoto is also well known for its hundreds of Buddhist temples and traditional Zen gardens. Many tourists visit the city every year on the Shinkansen or bullet train. It is particularly popular in spring when the cherry trees are in full blossom.

Kato-kun's mother and Bādo-kun are talking about Kyoto.

かとうくんの　おかあさん　：　これは　きょうとの　えはがきです。

バードくん　　　　　　　　　：　きょうとは　どんな　まちですか。

かとうくんの　おかあさん　：　きれいな　まちですよ。

バードくん　　　　　　　　　：　これは　なんですか。

かとうくんの　おかあさん　：　ゆうめいな　おてらです。

バードくん　　　　　　　　　：　この　えはがきを　ください。

かとうくんの　おかあさん　：　ええ、どうぞ。

VOCABULARY

おてら	temple	o-tera
えはがき	picture postcard	e-hagaki
え	picture	e
はがき	postcard	hagaki
よ	I tell you (particle)	yo

SHORT DIALOGUES

1

やまもとくんの　おかあさん　：　バードくんの　うちは　どこですか。

バードくん　　　　　　　　　：　コロラドです。

やまもとくんの　おかあさん　：　コロラドは　どんな　ところですか。

バードくん　　　　　　　　　：　とても　しずかな　ところです。

2

やまもとくんの　おかあさん　：　おちゃを　どうぞ。

バードくん　　　　　　　　　：　ありがとうございます。

やまもとくんの　おかあさん　：　おかしは　いかがですか。

バードくん　　　　　　　　　：　はい、いただきます。おいしいですね。

VOCABULARY

どこ	where	doko
とても	very	totemo
おかし	snacks (cakes, sweets, and savories)	o-kashi
いかがですか	How about…?	ikaga desu ka
いかが	how	ikaga
いただきます	eat (polite word for **tabemasu**)	itadakimasu
おいしいです	It tastes good.	oishii desu
おいしい	good, tasty (-i adj.)	oishii

QUIZ

`⊂ ⊃`

I. Make a statement as in the example.

ex. けんくん・げんき・おとこの　こ

→けんくんは　げんきな　おとこの　こです。

1. さくら・ゆうめい・はな

→ _____

2. きょうと・きれい・まち

→ _____

3. ナンシーさん・しんせつ・おんなの　こ

→ _____

`⊂ ⊃`

II. Write the appropriate Hiragana in the parentheses.
(If nothing is required, put an ✕ in the parentheses.)

1. これ（　　　）　50えん（　　　）　きってです。

2. きょうと（　　　）　ゆうめい（　　　）　まちです。

3. おおきい（　　　）　ジュース（　　　）　ください。

III. Answer the following questions as shown in the example.

ex. さくらは　どんな　はなですか。 　　　　　（きれい）

→きれいな　はなです。

1. みどりちゃんは　どんな　おんなの　こですか。 　　（げんき）

→

2. かとうくんの　おとうさんは　どんな　ひとですか。（しんせつ）

→

3. その　こうえんは　どんな　ところですか。 　　　（しずか）

→

4. その　やまは　どんな　やまですか。 　　　　　（ゆうめい）

→

5. その　かわは　どんな　かわですか。 　　　　　（きれい）

→

THE WEEKEND

あした えいがを みます。

KEY SENTENCES

1. バードくんは あした えいがを みます。
2. バードくんは まいあさ おちゃを のみます。
3. バードくんは ときどき かいものを します。
4. バードくんは あした べんきょうを しません。

1. Bādo-kun wa ashita ēga o mimasu.
2. Bādo-kun wa maiasa o-cha o nomimasu.
3. Bādo-kun wa tokidoki kaimono o shimasu.
4. Bādo-kun wa ashita benkyō o shimasen.

VOCABULARY

えいが	movie, cinema	ēga
みます（みる）	see (See SUMMARY TABLE on p.144)	mimasu (miru)
まいあさ	every morning	maiasa
まい〜	every	mai-
あさ	morning	asa
のみます（のむ）	drink	nomimasu (nomu)
ときどき	sometimes	tokidoki
かいものを します	shop	kaimono o shimasu
（かいものを する）		(kaimono o suru)
かいもの	shopping	kaimono
します（する）	do	shimasu (suru)
べんきょうを しません	do not study (See SUMMARY TABLE on p.144)	benkyō o shimasen
べんきょうを します	study	benkyō o shimasu
（べんきょうを する）		(benkyō o suru)
しません	do not do	shimasen

EXERCISES I

1. a. ex. たべます

b. ex. たべません

2. a. ex. ハンバーガー

   b. ex. バードくんは　ハンバーガーを　たべます。

3. **a. ex.** ジュース

　b. ex. かとうくんは　ジュースを　のみます。

4. **a. ex.** ほん

　b. ex. やまもとくんは　ほんを　よみます。

5. a. ex. えいが

   b. ex. きむらさんは　えいがを　みます。

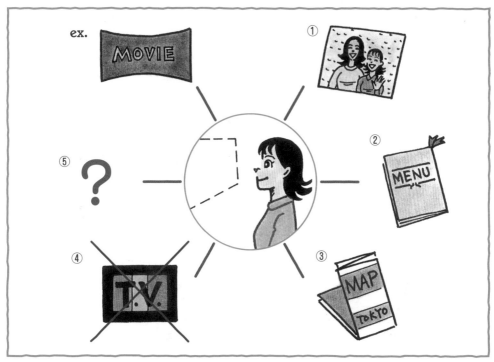

6. a. ex. おんがく

   b. ex. みどりちゃんは　おんがくを　ききます。

7. a. ex. ひらがな

   b. ex. バードくんは　ひらがなを　かきます。

8. a. ex. じしょ

   b. ex. たなかせんせいは　じしょを　かいます。

9. a. ex.　べんきょう

　　b. ex.　バードくんは　べんきょうを　します。

ex. ① ② ③ ④ ⑤

JAPAN NEWS

Enjoyed by adults, young people, and small children, there are "Manga" cartoons and comics in Japan about every subject you could possibly imagine. Boys read manga about robots and racers, college students dip into manga love stories, and businessmen learn how to use a new PC from a manga manual.

Famous manga comic strips include *Sazae-san*, a long-running newspaper serial about the life of a typical Japanese family, and *Doraemon*, a lovable cat robot from the future. Many Japanese manga comics like *Dragonball Z* and *Sailor Moon* have been made into animated TV series which are dubbed into different languages and shown all over the world. How many Japanese manga characters do you know?

EXERCISES II

1. ex. バードくんは　あした　ほんを　よみます。

あさって　てがみを　かきます。

	TOMORROW	THE DAY AFTER TOMORROW
ex.		
①		
②		
③		
④		

2. a. ex.

たなかせんせい：バードくんは　あした　ほんを　よみますか。

バードくん　　　：はい、よみます。

ex.

b. ex.

たなかせんせい：バードくんは　あさって　じゅうどうを　しますか。

バードくん　　　：いいえ、しません。

3. **ex.** バードくんは　まいあさ　ごはんを　たべます。

かとうくんは　まいあさ　たまごを　たべます。

やまもとくんは　まいあさ　パンを　たべます。

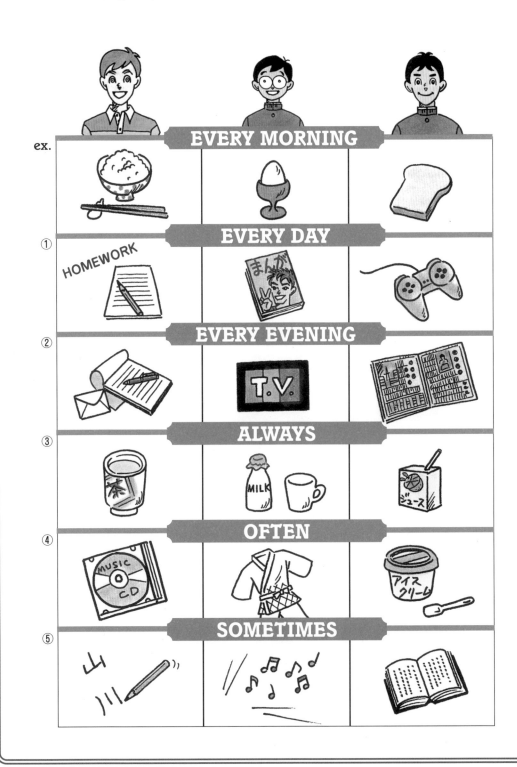

✰ VOCABULARY ✰

たべます（たべる）	eat	tabemasu (taberu)
よみます（よむ）	read	yomimasu (yomu)
ききます（きく）	listen	kikimasu (kiku)
かきます（かく）	write	kakimasu (kaku)
かいます（かう）	buy	kaimasu (kau)
サンドイッチ	sandwich	sandoitchi
スープ	soup	sūpu
くすり	medicine	kusuri
おさけ	saké, a liquor made from rice	o-sake
てがみ	letter	tegami
おもしろい	interesting (-i adj.)	omoshiroi
まんが	comic	manga
ちず	map	chizu
テレビ	television	terebi
カセット	cassette tape	kasetto
CD(シーディー)	compact disc	shiidii
あたらしい	new (-i adj.)	atarashii
ニュース	news	nyūsu
ひらがな	a phonetic writing system of Japanese, used for words of Japanese origin	Hiragana
かたかな	a phonetic writing system of Japanese, used for words of foreign origin	Katakana
かんじ	Chinese characters	Kanji
え	drawing	e
じしょ	dictionary	jisho
にく	meat	niku
たまご	egg	tamago
さかな	fish	sakana
じゅうどうを　します（じゅうどうを　する）	do judo	jūdō o shimasu (jūdō o suru)
しゅくだい	homework	shukudai
しゅくだいを　します（しゅくだいを　する）	do one's homework	shukudai o shimasu (shukudai o suru)
ファミコン	computer game machine	famikon
ファミコンを　します（ファミコンを　する）	play computer games	famikon o shimasu (famikon o suru)
ごはん	cooked rice	gohan
まいにち	every day	mainichi
まいばん	every evening, every night	maiban
ばん	evening	ban
いつも	always	itsumo
よく	often	yoku

MAIN DIALOGUE

Tanaka-sensē asks Bādo-kun about his plans for the weekend.

たなかせんせい： あしたは　やすみですね。　なにを　しますか。

バードくん　　　： かいものを　します。

たなかせんせい： いいですね。　なにを　かいますか。

バードくん　　　： あたらしい　じしょを　かいます。

☺ バードくんは　あした　かいものを　します。

VOCABULARY

いいですね	That's good.	ii desu ne
いい	good (-i adj.)	ii

SHORT DIALOGUES

1

バードくん　　　　：　まいあさ　なにを　たべますか。

たなかせんせい：　パンを　たべます。ときどき　ごはんも　たべます。

　　　　　　　　　　　バードくんは？

バードくん　　　　：　わたしは　いつも　ごはんを　たべます。

2

かとうくんの　おかあさん：　こんばん　ファミコンを　しますか。

バードくん　　　　　　　　　：　いいえ、しません。

かとうくんの　おかあさん：　じゃあ、いっしょに　この　ビデオを

　　　　　　　　　　　　　　　　　みましょう。

VOCABULARY

こんばん	this evening, tonight	komban
いっしょに	together	issho ni
ビデオ	video	bideo
みましょう	Let's watch.	mimashō

なにを　しますか。

Think of five things that you do every day and then five other things that you only do sometimes. First fill out the chart then practice saying the sentences.

ex.　まいにち　ごはんを　たべます。

　　　ときどき　えいがを　みます。

	まいにち	ときどき
ex.	ごはんを　たべます。	えいがを　みます。
1		
2		
3		
4		
5		

I. Match each object or activity with the most appropriate action.

ex. ほんを   ・ ききます

1. テレビを   ・   ・ たべます

2. ＣＤを   ・   ・ します

3. パンを   ・   ・ みます

4. べんきょうを   ・   よみます

5. じゅうどうを   ・   ・ ききます

6. じしょを   ・   ・ します

7. ニュースを   ・   ・ のみます

8. おちゃを   ・   ・ かいます

II. Make a statement as in the example.

ex. わたし・テレビ・みます

→わたしは　テレビを　みます。

1. おかあさん・おさけ・のみません

→ _____

2. かとうくん・まいにち・じゅうどう・します

→ _____

3. わたし・こんばん・ファミコン・しません

→ _____

4. バードくん・あした・じしょ・かいます

→ _____

◖ ◗

III. Complete the questions so that they fit the answers.

1. A：（　　　　　　　）　かいものを　しますか。

　　B：あした　します。

2. A：こんばん　（　　　　　　　）を　しますか。

　　B：おもしろい　テレビを　みます。

3. A：まいあさ　（　　　　　　　）を　のみますか。

　　B：コーヒーを　のみます。

◖ ◗

IV. Answer the following questions.

1. まいあさ　なにを　たべますか。

　　→ _____

2. まいあさ　なにを　のみますか。

　　→ _____

3. まいにち　テレビを　みますか。

　　→ _____

ほんやで　じしょを　かいました。

cc

KEY SENTENCES

1. バードくんは　ほんやで　じしょを　かいました。
2. おとうさんは　きのう　かいしゃの　しょくどうで
   ひるごはんを　たべませんでした。
3. バードくんは　きのう　6じに　おきました。

☆ VOCABULARY ☆

ほんや	bookstore	hon-ya
〜や	store, shop	-ya
で	at (particle)	de
かいました	bought (See SUMMARY TABLE on p.144)	kaimashita
しょくどう	cafeteria, canteen	shokudō
ひるごはん	lunch	hiru-gohan
たべませんでした	did not eat (See SUMMARY TABLE on p.144)	tabemasendeshita
に	on, at (particle)	ni
おきました	got up	okimashita
おきます（おきる）	get up	okimasu (okiru)

EXERCISES I

1. **a. ex.** きょうしつ

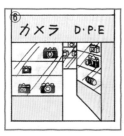
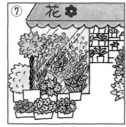

b. ex. あさごはん

2. **ex.** きょうしつで　べんきょうを　します。

ex.

①

②

③

④

⑤

⑥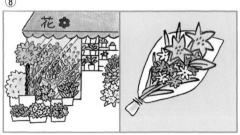

⑦

⑧

⑨

1. ex. バードくんは　きのう　ほんやで　じしょを　かいました。

おととい　デパートで　くつを　かいました。

	YESTERDAY	THE DAY BEFORE YESTERDAY
ex.		
①		
②		
③		
④		

2. a. ex.

たなかせんせい：バードくんは　きのう　じしょを　かいましたか。

バードくん　　　：はい、かいました。

ex.

たなかせんせい：バードくんは　おととい　テレビを　みましたか。

バードくん　　　：いいえ、みませんでした。

EXERCISES III

1. **ex.** バードくんは　7じに　おきました。

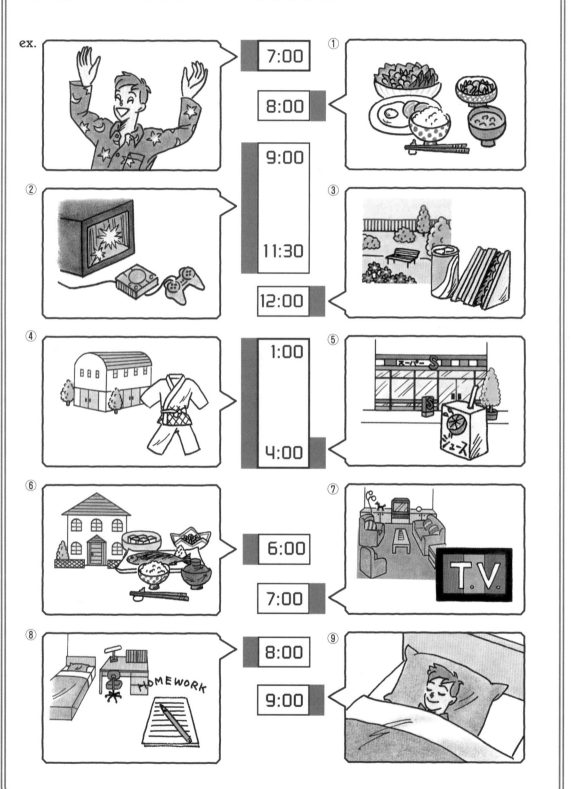

ex. — 7:00

① 8:00

② 9:00 — 11:30

③ 12:00

④ 1:00

⑤ 4:00

⑥ 6:00

⑦ 7:00

⑧ 8:00

⑨ 9:00

2. ex. A: かとうくんは げつようびに なにを しましたか。

B: たいいくかんで じゅうどうを しました。

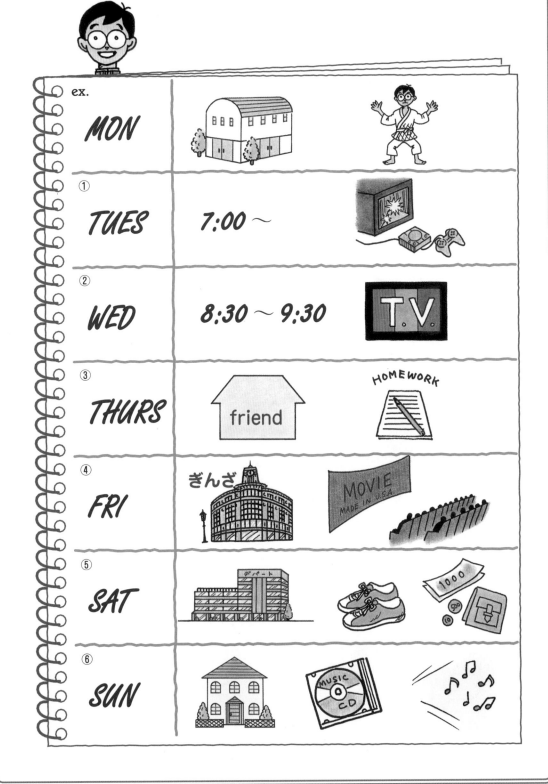

VOCABULARY

きょうしつ	classroom	kyōshitsu
たいいくかん	gymnasium	taiikukan
としょかん	library	toshokan
きっさてん	coffee shop	kissaten
ゆうびんきょく	post office	yūbinkyoku
カメラ	camera	kamera
へや	room	heya
いま	living room	ima
あさごはん	breakfast	asa-gohan
ばんごはん	dinner	ban-gohan
フィルム	film	firumu
でんち	battery	denchi
くつ	shoes	kutsu
かさ	umbrella	kasa
ねました	went to bed	nemashita
ねます（ねる）	go to bed	nemasu (neru)
ぎんざ	name of area in Tokyo	Ginza

SUMMARY TABLE

VERBS 1

*Verbs conjugation is not affected by the gender, number or person of the subject.
*Verbs conjugation shows only two tenses, the present form and the past form. Whether use of the present form refers to habitual action or the future, and whether the past form is equivalent to the English past tense, present perfect or past perfect can be determined from the context.

Present Form		Past Form	
aff.	*neg.*	*aff.*	*neg.*
たべます	たべません	たべました	たべませんでした
のみます	のみません	のみました	のみませんでした
よみます	よみません	よみました	よみませんでした
みます	みません	みました	みませんでした
ききます	ききません	ききました	ききませんでした
かきます	かきません	かきました	かきませんでした
かいます	かいません	かいました	かいませんでした
べんきょうを　します	べんきょうを　しません	べんきょうを　しました	べんきょうを　しませんでした
じゅうどうを　します	じゅうどうを　しません	じゅうどうを　しました	じゅうどうを　しませんでした
ファミコンを　します	ファミコンを　しません	ファミコンを　しました	ファミコンを　しませんでした
かいものを　します	かいものを　しません	かいものを　しました	かいものを　しませんでした
しゅくだいを　します	しゅくだいを　しません	しゅくだいを　しました	しゅくだいを　しませんでした
おきます	おきません	おきました	おきませんでした
ねます	ねません	ねました	ねませんでした

MAIN DIALOGUE

Tanaka-sensē asks Bādo-kun about last weekend.

たなかせんせい ： にちようびに　あたらしい　じしょを
　　　　　　　　　　かいましたか。

バードくん　　　 ： はい、かいました。

たなかせんせい ： どこで　かいましたか。

バードくん　　　 ： ぎんざの　ほんやで　かいました。
　　　　　　　　　　えいごの　ざっしも　かいました。

☺ バードくんは　にちようびに　ぎんざの　ほんやで
　じしょと　ざっしを　かいました。

SHORT DIALOGUES

1 バードくん ： おとうさんは どこで ひるごはんを
たべますか。

かとうくんの おとうさん ： たいてい かいしゃの しょくどうで
たべるよ。

2 きむらさん ： きのう なんじに おきた。

バードくん ： 6じに おきたよ。

きむらさん ： はやい。 わたしは 7じ。

3 やまもとくん ： どようびに おすもうさんを みたよ。

バードくん ： へえ、どこで。

やまもとくん ： とうきょうえきで。あくしゅを したよ。

JAPAN NEWS

Sumo wrestling is one of the oldest and most traditional of Japan's national sports. Wrestlers are enormous, weighing an average of 326 pounds or 148 kilograms, yet behind that layer of blubber is a thick but supple wall of muscle. After stamping their feet and throwing salt in the air, the wrestlers or rikishi push, shove, throw, trip and lift their opponents out of the ring or onto the ring's floor. Rikishi wear only loincloths when fighting. Their hair is tied up into a traditional chonmage top-knot.

VOCABULARY

たいてい	usually	taitē
たべる	eat (informal speech for **tabemasu**)	taberu
おきた	woke up (informal speech for **okimashita**)	okita
はやい	early (-i adj.)	hayai
おすもうさん	sumo wrestler	o-sumō-san
すもう	sumo	sumō
みた	saw (informal speech for **mimashita**)	mita
へえ	Is that right?	hē
とうきょうえき	Tokyo Station	Tōkyō-Eki
あくしゅを した	shook hands	akushu o shita
あくしゅ	shaking hands	akushu
した	did (informal speech for **shimashita**)	shita

T A S K ❽

どこで　しましたか。

I. Ask some friends questions like the one in the example so that you can complete all the information missing from the chart.

ex.

バードくん：スミスさんは　きのう　えいがを　みましたか。

スミスさん：はい、みました。

バードくん：どこで　みましたか。

スミスさん：ぎんざで　みました。

	ex.	1	2	3
	スミス さん/くん	＿＿＿＿ さん/くん	＿＿＿＿ さん/くん	＿＿＿＿ さん/くん
	きのう	きのうの　ばん	まいあさ	あした
	MOVIE			1000
	はい　いいえ	はい　いいえ	はい　いいえ	はい　いいえ
	ぎんざ	＿＿＿＿	＿＿＿＿	＿＿＿＿

II. Based on the information in the chart, make statements as shown in the example.

ex. スミスさんは　　きのう　　　　ぎんざで　えいがを　みました。

1. ＿＿＿＿＿＿＿　きのうの　ばん　＿＿＿＿＿＿＿＿＿＿＿＿＿＿＿

2. ＿＿＿＿＿＿＿　まいあさ　＿＿＿＿＿＿＿＿＿＿＿＿＿＿＿＿＿

3. ＿＿＿＿＿＿＿　あした

I. Write the appropriate particle in the parentheses.

(If nothing is required, put an × in the parentheses.)

1. わたし（　　　）まいあさ（　　　）6 じ（　　　）おきます。

2. おとうさん（　　　）ときどき（　　　）きっさてん（　　　）
コーヒー（　　　）のみます。

3. わたし（　　　）いつも（　　　）きょうしつ（　　　）
おべんとう（　　　）たべます。

4. バードくん（　　　）にちようび（　　　）ほんや（　　　）
じしょ（　　　）かいました。

II. Make statements as shown in the example.

ex. まいばん ・  ・テレビ・みます

→まいばん　へやで　テレビを　みます。

1. まいにち ・  ・べんきょう・します

→

2. きんようび ・  ・ほん・よみました

→

3. あした ・  ・きって・かいます

→

III. Complete the questions so that they fit the answers.

1. A：きのう　（　　　　　　）　に　ねましたか。
   B：10じに　ねました。

2. A：どようびに　（　　　　　　）　を　しましたか。
   B：はなやで　きれいな　はなを　かいました。

3. A：きょう　（　　　　　　）　で　ファミコンを　しますか。
   B：やまもとくんの　うちで　します。

IV. Answer the following questions.

1. まいあさ　なんじに　おきますか。

   →
   _____

2. まいにち　どこで　ひるごはんを　たべますか。

   →
   _____

3. いつ　しゅくだいを　しますか。

   →
   _____

4. まいばん　なんじに　ねますか。

   →
   _____

あした　きょうとへ　いきます。

KEY SENTENCES

1. おとうさんは　あした　きょうとへ　いきます。
2. この　バスは　とうきょうえきへ　いきません。
3. バードくんは　きょねん　アメリカから　にほんへ　きました。
4. バードくんは　らいねん　アメリカへ　かえります。

VOCABULARY

へ	to (particle) (See NOTE)	e
いきます（いく）	go (See SUMMARY TABLE on p.167)	ikimasu (iku)
バス	bus	basu
きょねん	last year	kyonen
から	from (particle)	kara
きました	came	kimashita
きます（くる）	come	kimasu (kuru)
らいねん	next year	rainen
かえります（かえる）	go back, return	kaerimasu (kaeru)

 NOTE The particle **e** which corresponds to the English preposition "to" can be used instead of **ni** in many sentences. Ex. Kyōto **e/ni** ikimasu.

EXERCISES I

ex. **a.** バードくんは　がっこうへ　いきます。

b. バードくんは　としょかんへ　いきます。

c. バードくんは　うちへ　かえります。

ex.

①

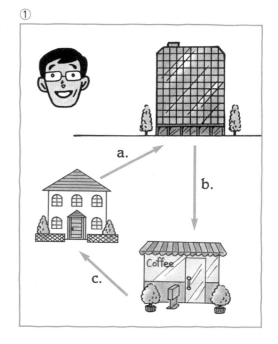

②

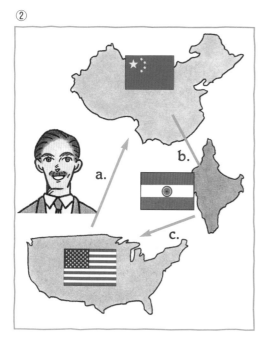

③

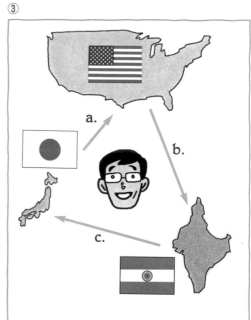

1. ex. がっこう

2. ex. バードくんは　がっこうへ　いきます。

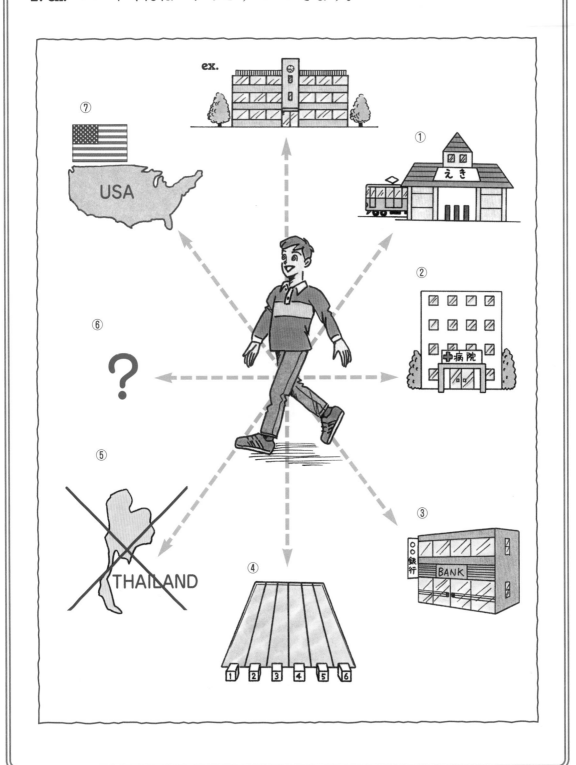

3. ex. バードくんは まいにち がっこうへ いきます。

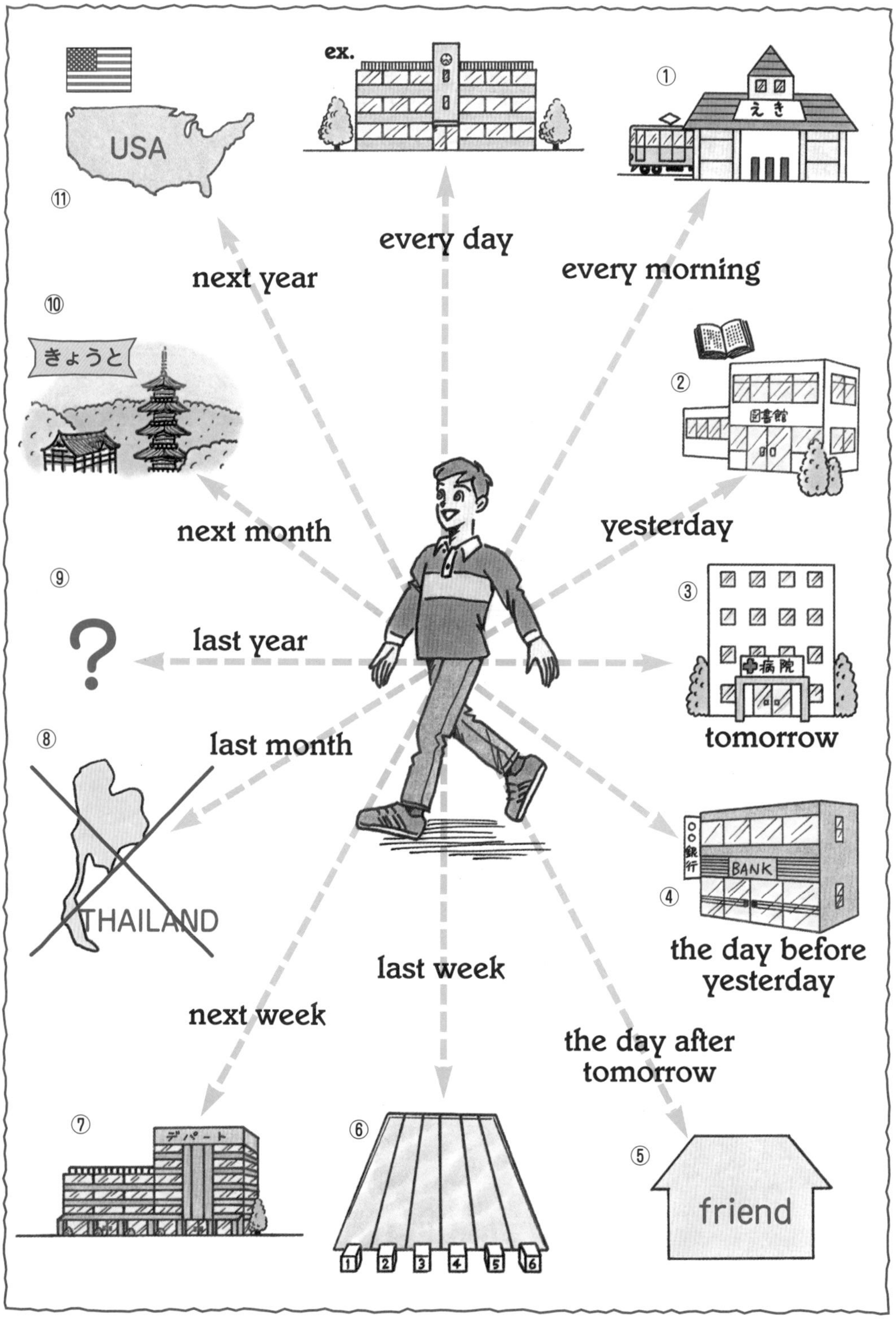

⑪ USA

ex.

① えき

next year

every day

every morning

⑩ きょうと

② 図書館

next month

yesterday

⑨ ?

③ 病院

last year

tomorrow

⑧ THAILAND

last month

④ BANK 銀行

the day before yesterday

next week

last week

the day after tomorrow

⑦ デパート

⑥ 1 2 3 4 5 6

⑤ friend

JAPAN NEWS

Whose turn is it to wash the dishes? Who has to polish the shoes this weekend? Sometimes the only fair way to decide something is by drawing lots. Japanese children, however, can always draw an "amida-kuji" game.

How to make an Amida-kuji

1. First draw a series of parallel vertical lines. Remember you will need at least one line for each person drawing a lot. There are five people (a, b, c, d, and e) in this amida-kuji.

2. Next draw horizontal lines to bridge the gaps between the vertical lines. It doesn't matter how many horizontal lines you draw or where you put them.

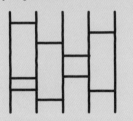

3. Finally, at the bottom of each vertical line write the name of the prize, or a number to show the order.

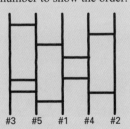

#3   #5   #1   #4   #2

How to play Amida-kuji

1. Cover the bottom part of the amida-kuji so that nobody can see the whole chart. You can also fold it over and over like a concertina.

2. Everyone chooses a vertical line and writes their name at the top of that line. After everyone has made their choice, unfold the amida-kuji so that all can see the chart clearly.

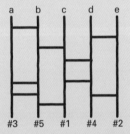

#3   #5   #1   #4   #2

3. Now, follow your vertical line, always moving from top to bottom. Remember that you are not allowed to go back on yourself.

4. When you come to a horizontal line you must follow it until you reach the next vertical line.

5. Continue this pattern until you reach the bottom.

The red arrows on our amida-kuji below show that C is the winner.
It doesn't matter how many vertical lines you draw or

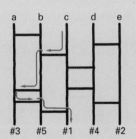

#3   #5   #1   #4   #2

where you put the horizontal lines. The top of each vertical line will lead to the bottom of only one vertical line and no two lines will ever finish in the same place.

Why not show you math teacher an amida-kuji and ask him or her to explain why?

Amida-kuji in this book

You have already met two amida-kuji in the Exercises section of this book. Do you remember this one from Lesson 2?

For the purposes of this book, we have turned our amida-kuji on its side so that the vertical lines are now horizontal and the horizontal lines are vertical. The rules are exactly the same as above except that you have to progress from left to right and you are allowed to move up or down the vertical lines until you reach the next horizontal line.

If you trace the pink line from the note pad in the example you will see that it belongs to Katō-kun's father.

Have fun with the amida-kuji in this book!

4. ex. A：バードくんは　どこへ　いきますか。

B：としょかんへ　いきます。

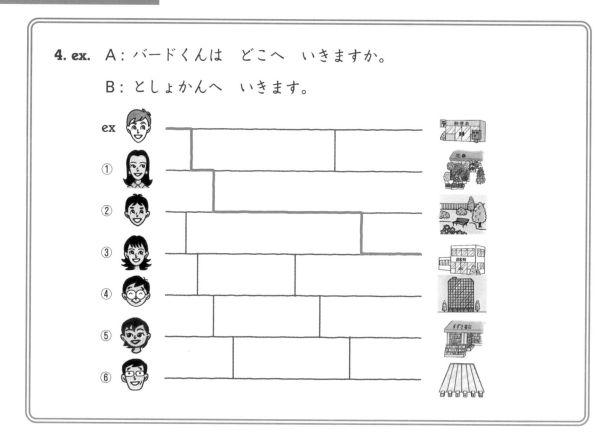

EXERCISES ⟨III⟩

1. a. ex. カナダから　にほんへ　きました。

b. ex. A：どこから　にほんへ　きましたか。

B：カナダから　きました。

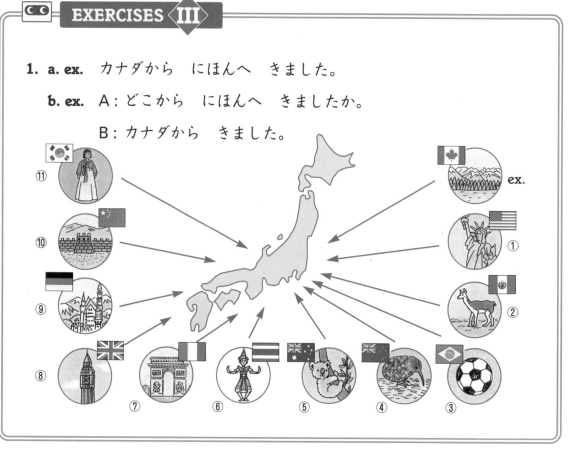

2.

a. ex. きょねん　カナダから　にほんへ　きました。

b. ex. A：いつ　カナダから　にほんへ　きましたか。

　　　　　B：きょねん　きました。

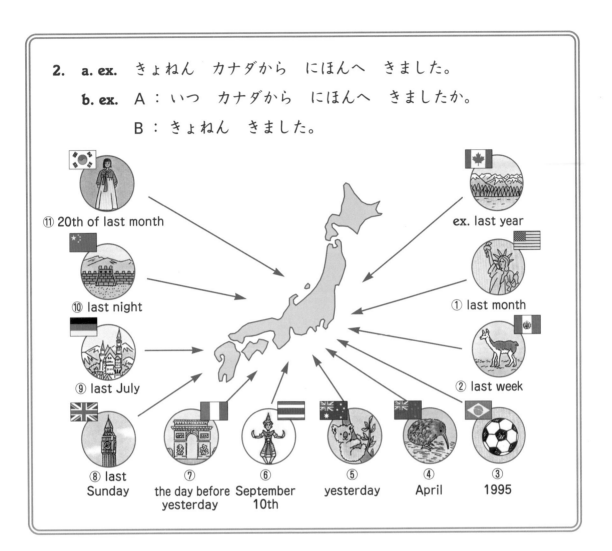

⑪ 20th of last month

⑩ last night

⑨ last July

⑧ last Sunday

⑦ the day before yesterday

⑥ September 10th

⑤ yesterday

④ April

③ 1995

② last week

① last month

ex. last year

⭐ VOCABULARY ⭐

えき	station	eki
びょういん	hospital	byōin
ぎんこう	bank	ginkō
プール	pool	pūru
タイ	Thailand	Tai
せんしゅう	last week (See SUMMARY TABLE on p.182)	sen-shū
らいしゅう	next week	rai-shū
らいげつ	next month	rai-getsu
せんげつ	last month	sen-getsu
ペルー	Peru	Perū
ニュージーランド	New Zealand	Nyūjiirando
かんこく	Republic of Korea	Kankoku

MAIN DIALOGUE

Katō-kun's mother sees Bādo-kun off at the entrance hall.

バードくん　　　　　　　　：いってきます。

かとうくんの　おかあさん：どこへ　いきますか。

バードくん　　　　　　　　：たなかせんせいの　うちへ　いきます。

かとうくんの　おかあさん：けんは？

バードくん　　　　　　　　：けんくんは　いきません。

かとうくんの　おかあさん：そう。　なんじごろ　かえりますか。

バードくん　　　　　　　　：5じごろ　かえります。

かとうくんの　おかあさん：いってらっしゃい。　きをつけて。

☺ バードくんは　たなかせんせいの　うちへ　いきます。
　　そして　5じごろ　かえります。

VOCABULARY

いってきます	Goodbye. (lit. I'm going and coming back.)	itte kimasu
	This is the reply to **itterasshai**.	
そう	Is that so?	sō
なんじごろ	about what time	nan-ji goro
〜ごろ	about	-goro
いってらっしゃい	Goodbye. (lit. Go and come back.)	itterasshai
	Said to members of a household	
	as they leave the house.	
きをつけて	Take care.	ki o tsukete
そして	and then	soshite

① I'm off then.

② · · · · · ?

③

④ ?

⑤ No.

⑥ · · · · · · · · ?

⑦ about

⑧ Bye.

SHORT DIALOGUES

1

みどりちゃん　　：あした　なんじに　がっこうへ　いく。

バードくん　　　：8じに　いくよ。

みどりちゃん　　：じゃあ、わたしも　8じに　いく。

2

バードくん　　　：すみません、この　バスは　とうきょうえきへ
　　　　　　　　　いきますか。

おんなの　ひと：いいえ、いきません。

バードくん　　　：どの　バスが　いきますか。

おんなの　ひと：あの　1ばんの　バスが　いきます。

VOCABULARY

いく	go (informal speech for ikimasu)	iku
1ばん	No.1	ichi-ban
が	(subject marker, particle)	ga

I. Write the appropriate particle in the parentheses.

(If nothing is required, put an ✕ in the parentheses.)

1. バードくんは　きょねん（　　　）にほん（　　　）きました。

2. バードくんは　8がつ（　　　）アメリカ（　　　）きました。

3. バードくんは　らいねん（　　　）8がつ（　　　）
   アメリカ（　　　）かえります。

4. バードくんは　まいにち（　　　）がっこう（　　　）いきます。

5. バードくんは　にちようび（　　　）デパート（　　　）
   くつ（　　　）かいました。

II. Change the following sentences as in the example.

ex.　わたしは　あした　　　　　　　いきます。　　　　（きのう）

→わたしは　きのう　ぎんこうへ　いきました。

1. わたしは　せんしゅう　　　　　　　いきました。　（らいしゅう）

→ _____

2. わたしは　らいげつ　きょうと　　　いきます。　　（せんげつ）

→ _____

3. ちちは　きょねん　　　　　　　きました。　　　（らいねん）

→ _____

III. Complete the questions so that they fit the answers.

1. A：バードくんは　（　　　　　　）から　きましたか。

   B：アメリカから　きました。

2. A：おかあさんは　（　　　　　）に　デパートへ　いきますか。

   B：にちようびに　いきます。

3. A：おとうさんは　（　　　　　）きょうとへ　いきますか。

   B：どようびに　いきます。

4. A：きのう　（　　　　　）に　うちへ　かえりましたか。

   B：4じに　かえりました。

5. A：あした　（　　　　　）を　しますか。

   B：プールへ　いきます。

IV. Answer the following questions.

1. たいてい　なんじに　うちへ　かえりますか。

   →＿＿＿＿＿＿＿＿＿＿＿＿＿＿＿＿＿＿＿＿＿

2. あした　としょかんへ　いきますか。

   →＿＿＿＿＿＿＿＿＿＿＿＿＿＿＿＿＿＿＿＿＿

3. にちようびに　どこへ　いきますか。

   →＿＿＿＿＿＿＿＿＿＿＿＿＿＿＿＿＿＿＿＿＿

GOING BY BUS

バスで がっこうへ いきます。

KEY SENTENCES

1. バードくんは バスで がっこうへ いきます。
2. わたしは あるいて えきへ いきます。

⭐ VOCABULARY ⭐

で	by (particle)	de
あるいて	on foot, walking	aruite

EXERCISES I

1. **ex.** バイク

2. **ex.** バードくんは　じてんしゃで　こうえんへ　いきます。

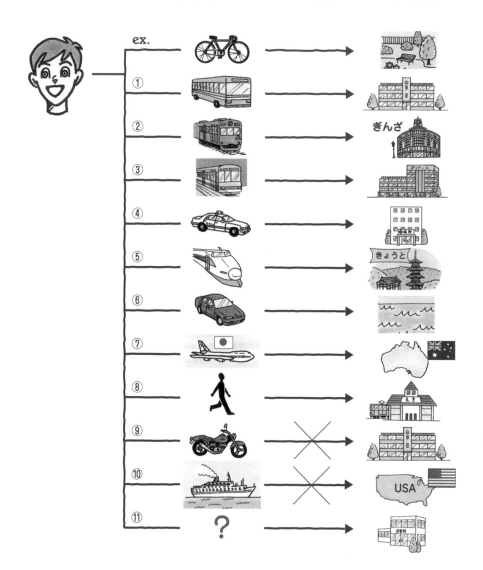

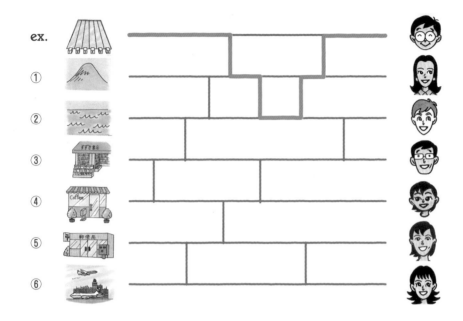

1. ex. A: だれが プールへ いきましたか。

B: かとうくんが いきました。

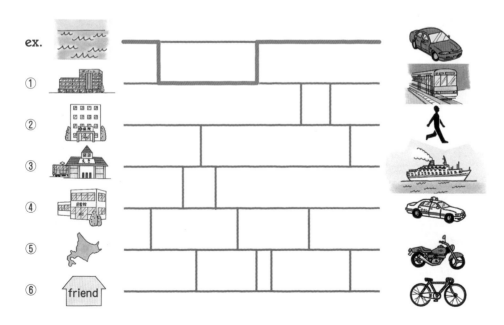

2. ex. A: なんで うみへ いきましたか。

B: くるまで いきました。

EXERCISES III

ex. かとうくんは　いつも　あるいて　えきへ　いきます。

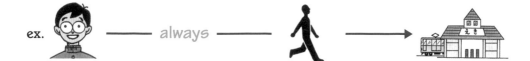

ex. — always —

① — usually —

② — tomorrow —

③ — often —

④ — 10th of last month —

⑤ — the day after tomorrow —

⑥ — next Sunday —

⑦ — last night —

⑧ — last Saturday —

⑨ — sometimes —

きょうと

USA

friend

?

★ VOCABULARY ★

バイク	motorbike	baiku
でんしゃ	train	densha
しんかんせん	"Shinkansen" Bullet train	Shinkansen
ちかてつ	subway, underground railway	chikatetsu
タクシー	taxi	takushii
ひこうき	airplane	hikōki
ふね	ship, boat	fune
くうこう	airport	kūkō
ほっかいどう	name of island north of Honshu	Hokkaidō

SUMMARY TABLE •

Present Form		Past Form	
aff.	*neg.*	*aff.*	*neg.*
いきます	いきません	いきました	いきませんでした
きます	きません	きました	きませんでした
かえります	かえりません	かえりました	かえりませんでした

MAIN DIALOGUE

Bādo-kun tells Tanaka-sensē that he will go to the airport in Katō-kun's father's car.

たなかせんせい ： バードくんの　おとうさんは　いつ　にほんへ
　　　　　　　　　　きますか。

バードくん　　　 ： らいしゅうの　どようびに　きます。

たなかせんせい ： バードくんは　くうこうへ　いきますか。

バードくん　　　 ： はい、かとうくんの　おとうさんの　くるまで
　　　　　　　　　　いきます。

☺ バードくんは　どようびに　かとうくんの　おとうさんの
　くるまで　くうこうへ　いきます。

SHORT DIALOGUES

1

せんせい　　　：　おとうさんは　もう　アメリカへ　かえりましたか。

バードくん　　：　はい、かえりました。

せんせい　　　：　いつ　かえりましたか。

バードくん　　：　おととい　かえりました。

2

たなかせんせい：もう　とうきょうディズニーランドへ　いきましたか。

バードくん　　　：いいえ、まだです。

3

バードくん　　　：こんにちは。

たなかせんせい：いらっしゃい。　どうぞ　おあがりください。

バードくん　　　：おじゃまします。

VOCABULARY

もう	already	mō
とうきょうディズニーランド	Tokyo Disneyland	Tōkyō Dizuniirando
まだです	Not yet.	mada desu
まだ	yet	mada
いらっしゃい	Come in.	irasshai
	(Less formal than **irasshaimase**)	
おあがりください	Please come in.	o-agari kudasai
	(used at the entrance to one's house)	
おじゃまします	Sorry to intrude.	o-jama shimasu
（おじゃまする）		o-jama suru

QUIZ

▭▭

I. Write the appropriate particle in the parentheses.
(If nothing is required, put an ✕ in the parentheses.)

1. わたしは　まいあさ（　　　）ちかてつ（　　　）
   がっこう（　　　）いきます。

2. わたしは　せんしゅう（　　　）にちようび（　　　）
   バス（　　　）くうこう（　　　）いきました。

3. おかあさんは　いつも（　　　）あるいて（　　　）
   スーパー（　　　）いきます。

4. バードくんの　おとうさんは　8がつ（　　　）
   ひこうき（　　　）　アメリカ（　　　）きます。

▭▭

II. Change the following sentences as in the example.

ex. おとうさんは　まいにち　かいしゃへ　いきます。　（ 🚗 ）
   →おとうさんは　まいにち　くるまで　かいしゃへ　いきます。

1. わたしは　きょう　ともだちの　うちへ　いきます。（ 🚶 ）
   →_____

2. わたしは　きのう　としょかんへ　いきました。　　（ 🚲 ）
   →_____

3. おかあさんは　にちようびに　デパートへ　いきました。（ 🚌 ）
   →_____

III. Complete the questions so that they fit the answers.

1. A:（　　　　　　）で　きましたか。

   B:バスで　きました。

2. A:（　　　　　　）へ　いきますか。

   B:ほっかいどうへ　いきます。

3. A:（　　　　　　）　アメリカへ　かえりますか。

   B:らいねんの　3がつに　かえります。

4. A:（　　　　　　）が　ゆうびんきょくへ　いきますか。

   B:みどりちゃんが　いきます。

IV. Answer the following questions.

1. まいにち　なんで　うちへ　かえりますか。

   → _____

2. おとうさんは　いつも　バスで　かいしゃへ　いきますか。

   → _____

3. どようびに　どこへ　いきますか。

   → _____

   なんで　いきますか。

   → _____

まいにち　かとうくんと　がっこうへ　いきます。

KEY SENTENCES

1. バードくんは　まいにち　かとうくんと　がっこうへ　いきます。

2. バードくんは　ことしの　8がつに　ひとりで　にほんへ　きました。

3. バードくんは　きのう　どこも　いきませんでした。

☆ V O C A B U L A R Y ☆

ことし	this year	kotoshi
ひとりで	alone	hitori de
どこも…ません	go …anywhere	doko mo…masen
どこも	nowhere	doko mo

EXERCISES I

1. ex. バードくんは　かとうくんと　がっこうへ　いきます。

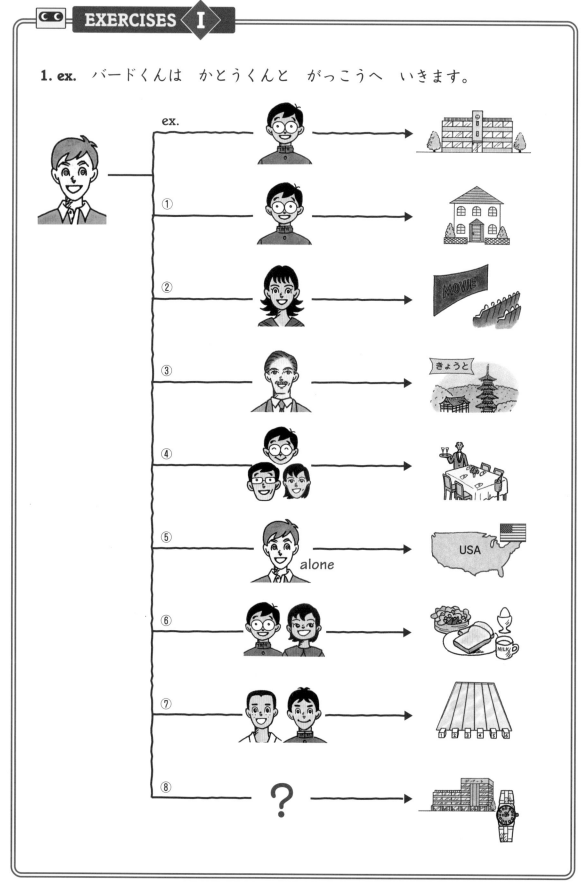

ex.

①

②

③

④

⑤ alone

⑥

⑦

⑧ ?

2. ex. バードくんは　まいあさ　かとうくんと　がっこうへ　いきます。

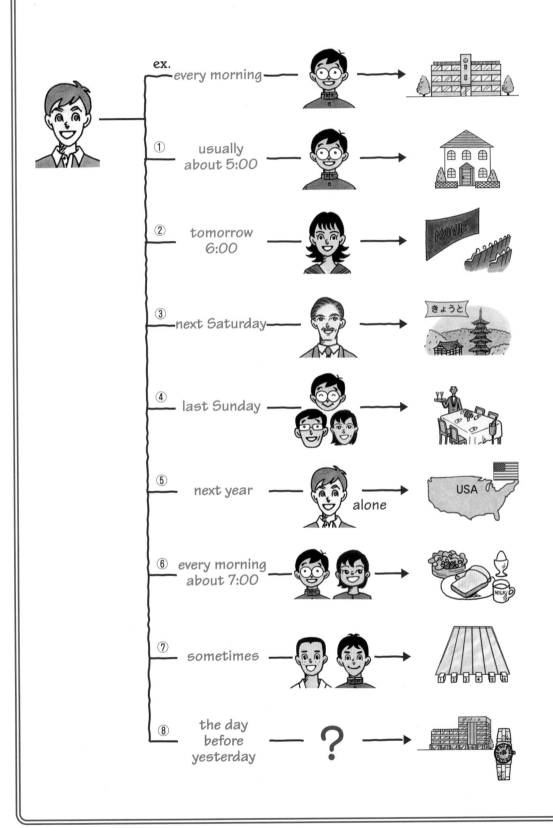

ex. every morning

① usually about 5:00

② tomorrow 6:00

③ next Saturday

④ last Sunday

⑤ next year — alone

⑥ every morning about 7:00

⑦ sometimes

⑧ the day before yesterday ？

EXERCISES II

ex. バードくんは　なにも　たべません。

バードくんは　どこも　いきません。

ex.

friend

①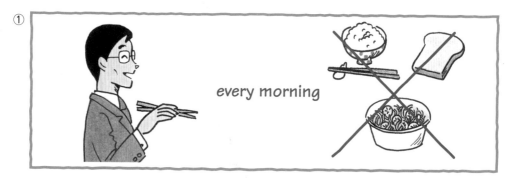
every morning

②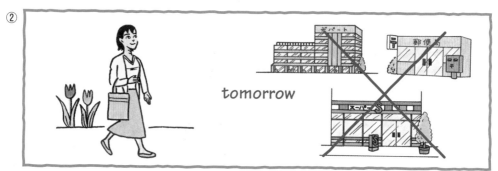
tomorrow

③
last night

VOCABULARY

せんぱい	one's senior (See NOTE)	sempai
けさ	this morning	kesa
なにも…ません	do…anything	nani mo…masen
なにも	nothing	nani mo

 A **sempai** or senior plays an important role in Japanese society and can refer to anyone who has enrolled at a school or joined a company before you. When speaking to a **sempai** you should use formal speech even though your **sempai** will probably use informal speech. This is illustrated in the second Short Dialogue on page 180.

MAIN DIALOGUE

Katō-kun's mother asks Bādo-kun about his plans for tomorrow.

バードくん ： ただいま。

かとうくんの　おかあさん ： おかえりなさい。

バードくん ： あした　どうぶつえんへ　いきます。

かとうくんの　おかあさん ： だれと　いきますか。

バードくん ： やまもとくんと　きむらさんと
　　　　　　　　　　　　　いきます。

かとうくんの　おかあさん ： たなかせんせいも　いきますか。

バードくん ： はい、いきます。

☺ バードくんは　あした　たなかせんせいと　ともだちと
どうぶつえんへ　いきます。

JAPAN NEWS

Remember never to enter a Japanese home with your shoes on! All apartments and houses in Japan are fitted with a special hall where you can take off your outdoor footwear. Step up and no doubt there will be a pair of house slippers –special ones for guests– to wear when you walk around carpeted and wood-tiled rooms. Another pair of slippers– usually made of washable plastic– will be provided in the bathroom, so you don't have to wear your house slippers when going to the toilet. Only stocking-clad or bare feet are allowed in Japanese-style *tatami* rooms.

VOCABULARY

ただいま	I'm back.	tadaima
おかえりなさい	Welcome back.	o-kaerinasai
どうぶつえん	zoo	dōbutsuen

SHORT DIALOGUES

1

たなかせんせい ： おねえさんは　いつ　にほんへ　きますか。

バードくん ： らいねんの　なつやすみに　きます。

たなかせんせい ： おかあさんも　きますか。

バードくん ： いいえ、ははは　きません。
　　　　　　　　　あねは　ひとりで　きます。

2

せんぱい ： あした　れんしゅうを　する。

バードくん ： はい、します。

せんぱい ： だれと　する。

バードくん ： やまもとくんと　します。

3

バードくん ： きのう　かとうくんの　おかあさんと　ぎんざの
　　　　　　　　デパートへ　いきました。

たなかせんせい ： バードくんは　なにを　かいましたか。

バードくん ： なにも　かいませんでした。

VOCABULARY

れんしゅうを　する	practice (informal speech for renshū o shimasu)	renshū o suru
れんしゅう	practice	renshū
する	do	suru

TASK 9

どの えですか。

Choose the most appropriate picture for each sentence.

ex. デパートへ いきました。 ひとりで いきました。 なにも かいませんでした。

①  ②  ③  ④

( )   ( )   ( )   (◯)

1. くるまで うみへ いきました。 とても きれいな うみでした。
ともだちと サッカーを しました。*1

①  ②  ③  ④

( )   ( )   ( )   ( )

2. 7がつ ようかは たんじょうびでした。 プレゼント*2は カメラでした。
おおきい ケーキを たべました。

①  ②  ③  ④

( )   ( )   ( )   ( )

3. どうぶつえんへ いきました。 そして、きっさてんで アイスクリームを
たべました。 みどりちゃんは いきませんでした。

①  ②  ③  ④

( )   ( )   ( )   ( )

*1 サッカーを します（サッカーを する）　play soccer　sakkā o shimasu (sakkā o suru)
*2 プレゼント　　　　　　　　　　　　　 gift　purezento

SUMMARY TABLE ●

RELATIVE TIME EXPRESSIONS 1

Day	おととい day before yesterday	きのう yesterday	きょう today	あした tomorrow	あさって day after tomorrow	まいにち every day
Week	せんせんしゅう week before last	せんしゅう last week	こんしゅう this week	らいしゅう next week	さらいしゅう week after next	まいしゅう every week
Month	せんせんげつ month before last	せんげつ last month	こんげつ this month	らいげつ next month	さらいげつ month after next	まいつき every month
Year	おととし year before last	きょねん last year	ことし this year	らいねん next year	さらいねん year after next	まいねん every year

RELATIVE TIME EXPRESSIONS 2

Morning	おとといの あさ morning before last	きのうの あさ yesterday morning	けさ this morning	あしたの あさ tomorrow morning	あさっての あさ morning of the day after tomorrow	まいあさ every morning
Evening	おとといの ばん/よる evening/night before last	きのうの ばん/よる yesterday evening/night	こんばん this evening tonight	あしたの ばん/よる tomorrow evening/night	あさっての ばん/よる evening/night the day after tomorrow	まいばん every evening

I. Write the appropriate particles in the parentheses.

(If a particle is not required, put an ✕ in the parentheses.)

1. わたしは　まいあさ（　　　）ともだち（　　　）
   がっこう（　　　）いきます。

2. わたしは　まいにち（　　　）せんぱい（　　　）
   サッカー（　　　）します。

3. せんしゅう（　　　）どようび（　　　）ひとり（　　　）
   かいもの（　　　）　しました。

4. きのう（　　　）デパート（　　　）なに（　　　）
   かいませんでした。

5. らいしゅう（　　　）どようび（　　　）どこ（　　　）
   いきません。

II. Change the following sentences as in the example.

ex. わたしは　きのう　ゆうびんきょくへ　いきました。（おかあさん）

→わたしは　きのう　おかあさんと　ゆうびんきょくへ　いきました。

1. バードくんは　らいねん　アメリカへ　かえります。　（ひこうき）

　　→

2. わたしは　きのう　しょくどうで　ひるごはんを　たべました。

（ともだち）

　　→

3. わたしは　ときどき　としょかんで　ほんを　よみます。　（ひとり）

　　→

4. きのう　デパートで　ともだちと　CDを　かいました。（やすい）

　　→

III. Complete the questions so that they fit the answers.

1. A：きのう　（　　　　　　　）へ　いきましたか。

　　B：どうぶつえんへ　いきました。

2. A：（　　　　　　　）と　こうえんへ　いきましたか。

　　B：せんぱいと　いきました。

3. A：たいいくかんで　（　　　　　　　）を　しましたか。

　　B：じゅうどうを　しました。

IV. Answer the following questions.

1. いつも　きょうしつで　ひるごはんを　たべますか。

→ _____

2. たいてい　だれと　ひるごはんを　たべますか。

→ _____

3. いつも　ひとりで　うちへ　かえりますか。

→ _____

4. にちようびに　なにを　しますか。

→ _____

べんきょうの あとで じゅうどうを します。

MAIN TEXT

　バードくんは　アメリカじんです。
ことしの　8がつに　ひとりで
にほんへ　きました。
バードくんは　いま　かとうくんの　うちに　います。

　　　　　まいあさ　6じはんに　おきます。
あさごはんの　まえに　すこし
ジョギングを　します。
7じ45ふんに　かとうくんと
バスで　がっこうへ　いきます。

がっこうは　8じはんから　3じ40ぷんまでです。
まいにち　にほんごや　れきしや
りかの　べんきょうを　します。
ときどき　かんじが　わかりませんが、
べんきょうは　おもしろいです。
せんせいや　ともだちは　とても
しんせつです。

べんきょうの　あとで　せんぱいや
やまもとくんと　じゅうどうを　します。
まいばん　かとうくんと　いっしょに
しゅくだいを　します。　そして
10じごろ　ねます。

あしたは　どようびですから、
がっこうは　12じまでです。　ごご
かとうくんと　やまもとくんの
うちへ　いきます。　そして
ファミコンを　します。

⭐ VOCABULARY ⭐

います　（いる）	stay	imasu (iru)
〜の　まえに	before ...	...no mae ni
すこし	a little	sukoshi
ジョギングを　します（ジョギングを　する）	jog	jogingu o shimasu (jogingu o suru)
ジョギング	jogging	jogingu
や	and etc. (particle)	ya
わかりません	do not understand	wakarimasen
わかります　（わかる）	understand	wakarimasu (wakaru)
＿＿＿が	...but (particle)	...ga
おもしろいです	is interesting	omoshiroi desu
しんせつです	is/are kind	shinsetsu desu
〜の　あとで	after ...	...no ato de
＿＿＿から	because (particle)...	...kara

EXERCISES Ⅰ

1. ex. A：バードくんは　いつ　じゅうどうを　しますか。

B：べんきょうの　あとで　します。

＊バードくんは　べんきょうの　あとで　じゅうどうを　します。

ex.

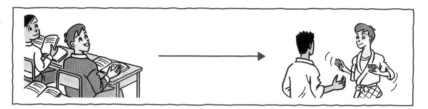

①

②

③

④

⑤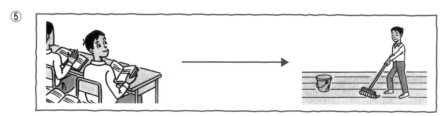

2. ex. A：バードくんは　いつ　ジョギングを　しますか。

あさごはんの　まえに　しますか、あとで　しますか。

B：あさごはんの　まえに　ジョギングを　します。

＊バードくんは　あさごはんの　まえに　ジョギングを　します。

ex.

①

②

③

④

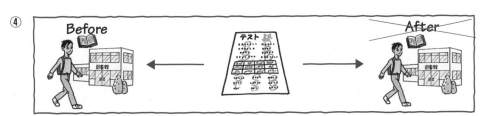

⑤

EXERCISES II

ex. バードくんは けさ パンと たまごを たべました。

かとうくんは けさ パンや たまごを たべました。

ex.

①

②

③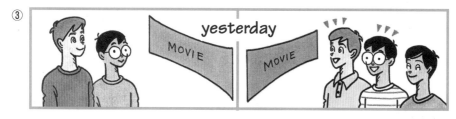

④

⑤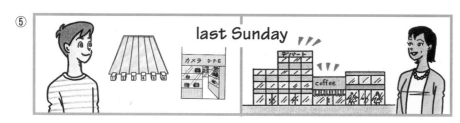

ex. バードくんは　アメリカじんです。

T A S K ⑩

いい　こですか、わるい　こですか。

Answer the following questions circling the letter of the sentence that suits you best.

1. まいあさ　なんじに　おきますか。
　　ア　6じごろ　おきます。
　　イ　7じごろ　おきます。
　　ウ　8じごろ　おきます。

2. まいあさ　ごはんを　たべますか。
　　ア　まいあさ　たべます。
　　イ　ときどき　たべます。
　　ウ　あまり　たべません。*1

3. ミルクを　のみますか。
　　ア　よく　のみます。
　　イ　ときどき　のみます。
　　ウ　あまり　のみません。

4. やさいを　たべますか。
　　ア　まいにち　たべます。
　　イ　ときどき　たべます。
　　ウ　あまり　たべません。

5. おかしを　たべますか。
　　ア　あまり　たべません。
　　イ　ときどき　たべます。
　　ウ　よく　たべます。

6. しゅくだいを　しますか。
　　ア　いつも　します。
　　イ　ときどき　します。
　　ウ　あまり　しません。

7. スポーツを　しますか。
　　ア　よく　します。
　　イ　ときどき　します。
　　ウ　ぜんぜん　しません。*2

8. まいばん　なんじに　ねますか。
　　ア　10じまえ*3に　ねます。
　　イ　10じから　11じの　あいだ*4に
　　　　ねます。
　　ウ　11じすぎ*5に　ねます。

*1 あまり…ません	not very...	amari...masen
*2 ぜんぜん…ません	not ever...	zenzen...masen
*3 〜まえ	before...	mae
*4 あいだ	between	aida
*5 〜すぎ	after...	sugi

Calculate your score based on the following:
（ア: **3 points**, イ: **2 points**, ウ: **1 point**）.

1	2	3	4	5	6	7	8	TOTAL

★　★　★　★　★　★　どんな　こですか。★　★　★　★　★　★

21〜24 points:　とても　いい　こです。
17〜20 points:　いい　こです。
13〜16 points:　あまり　いい　こではありません。
　8〜12 points:　わるい*6　こです。

*6 わるい　bad　warui

Q U I Z

I. True or false?

Reading the Main Text, check the accuracy of each statement below. If true, then write a ◯, and if false, write an ✕ in the parentheses.

1. (　　) バードくんは　アメリカから　にほんへ　きました。

2. (　　) バードくんは　おとうさんと　にほんへ　きました。

3. (　　) バードくんは　いま　やまもとくんの　うちに　います。

4. (　　) バードくんは　まいあさ　バスで　がっこうへ　いきます。

5. (　　) バードくんは　まいあさ　ひとりで　がっこうへ　いきます。

6. (　　) バードくんは　まいにち　れきしや　りかの　べんきょうを　します。

7. (　　) バードくんの　ともだちは　あまり　しんせつではありません。

8. (　　) バードくんは　まいあさ　かとうくんと　しゅくだいを　します。

9. (　　) バードくんは　どようびに　がっこうへ　いきません。

10. (　　) バードくんは　あした　やまもとくんの　うちへ　いきます。

QUIZ

II. Read the Main Text once again and answer the following questions.

1. バードくんは　いつ　にほんへ　きましたか。

    → _____

2. バードくんは　まいあさ　6じに　おきますか。

    → _____

3. バードくんは　あさごはんの　まえに　なにを　しますか。

    → _____

4. バードくんは　なんじに　がっこうへ　いきますか。

    → _____

5. がっこうは　8じはんから　なんじまでですか。

    → _____

6. がっこうの　べんきょうは　どうですか。

    → _____

7. バードくんは　べんきょうの　あとで　なにを　しますか。

    → _____

8. バードくんは　あさ　しゅくだいを　しますか。

    → _____

9. バードくんは　まいばん　なんじに　ねますか。

    → _____

10. バードくんは　あした　なにを　しますか。

    → _____

Grammar Review

and

Mini Dictionary
ちいさいじしょ

Grammar Review

A Sentence Patterns

Sentence patterns	Examples	Lesson
1.……は……です	1. わたしは　バードです。	1
	2. がっこうの　でんわばんごうは　3459-9620です。	2
	3. ひるやすみは　12じから　1じまでです。	3
	4. かいしゃの　やすみは　どようびと　にちようびです。	4
	5. さくらは　きれいな　はなです。	9
2.……を　ください	1. これを　ください。	6
	2. その　りんごを　みっつ　ください。	7
3.……を　おねがいします	あかい　ペンを　1ぽん　おねがいします。	8
4.……で　おねがいします	1000えんで　おねがいします。	8
5.……を　―ます	バードくんは　あした　えいがを　みます。	10
6.……で　……を　―ます	バードくんは　ほんやで　じしょを　かいました。	11
7.……に　―ます	バードくんは　きのう　6じに　おきました。	11
8.……へ／に　―ます	おとうさんは　あした　きょうとへ　いきます。	12
9.……で　……へ／に　―ます	バードくんは　バスで　がっこうへ　いきます。	13
10.―ましょう	いっしょに　この　ビデオを　みましょう。	10
11.―てください	ちょっと　まってください。	Useful Expressions

B Interrogatives

Interrogatives	Examples	Lesson
1. なん	これは　なんですか。	2
なんばん	がっこうの　でんわばんごうは　なんばんですか。	2
なんじ	いま　なんじですか。	3
なんじから	スーパーは　なんじからですか。	3
なんじまで	スーパーは　なんじまでですか。	3
なんじに	まいあさ　なんじに　おきますか。	11
なんようび	きょうは　なんようびですか。	4
なんさい	バードくんは　なんさいですか。	5
なんがつ	きのうは　なんがつ　なんにちでしたか。	5
なんにち	きのうは　なんがつ　なんにちでしたか。	5
なんの	なんの　ざっし。	8
なんまい	A：かみを　ください。	
	B：なんまいですか。	7
なんぼん	A：えんぴつを　ください。	
	B：なんぼんですか。	7
なんで	なんで　うみへ　いきましたか。	13
なに	これは　なに。	2
なにを	あした　なにを　しますか。	10
2. だれ／どなた	この　おんなの　ひとは　だれ／どなたですか。	7
だれの	だれの　ノートですか。	2
だれと	バードくんは　まいあさ　だれと　がっこうへ　いきますか。	14
3. いつ	バードくんの　たんじょうびは　いつですか。	5
4. いくら	トマトは　いくらですか。	6

Interrogatives	Examples	Lesson
5. いくつ	A：りんごを　ください。	
	B：いくつですか。	7
6. どれ	バードくんの　じてんしゃは　どれですか。	6
7. どの	A：えんぴつを　ください。	
	B：どの　えんぴつですか。	7
8. どこ	バードくんの　うちは　どこですか。	9
どこの	これは　どこの　とけいですか。	7
どこで	まいにち　どこで　ひるごはんを　たべますか。	11
どこへ	バードくんは　あした　どこへ　いきますか。	12
どこから	バードくんは　どこから　にほんへ　きましたか。	12
9. どんな	きょうとは　どんな　まちですか。	9

C Verbs & Adjectives

Lesson	Verbs	ーい adjectives	ーな adjectives
Useful Expressions	かします（かす）lend まちます（まつ）wait		
5		あぶない　dangerous	だいじょうぶな　OK, all right
6	みせます（みせる）show		
8		あおい　blue あかい　red おおきい　big くろい　black しろい　white たかい　expensive ちいさい　small やすい　cheap	
9	いただきます（いただく） 　　　　　　　receive	おいしい　tasty, delicious	きれいな　pretty, beautiful, clean げんきな　healthy, cheerful しずかな　quiet しんせつな　kind ゆうめいな　famous
10	かいます（かう）buy かきます（かく）write, draw ききます（きく）listen します*（する）do たべます（たべる）eat のみます（のむ）drink みます　（みる）see よみます（よむ）read	あたらしい　new いい　good おもしろい　interesting	
11	おきます（おきる）get up ねます　（ねる）go to bed	はやい　early	
12	いきます　（いく）go かえります（かえる）return きます　　（くる）come		
15	います　（いる）stay わかります（わかる）understand	わるい　bad	

＊The following is a selection of compounds that are formed with します.

あくしゅを　します	shake hands	Lesson 11
かいものを　します	go shopping	Lesson 10
サッカーを　します	play soccer	Lesson 4
しゅくだいを　します	do homework	Lesson 10
じゅうどうを　します	do judo	Lesson 10
ジョギングを　します	jog	Lesson 15
ファミコンを　します	play computer games	Lesson 10
べんきょうを　します	study	Lesson 10
れんしゅうを　します	practice	Lesson 14

D Particles

Particles	Examples	Lesson
は	1. わたしは　バードです。	1
	2. きょうは　にちようびです。	4
	3. さくらは　きれいな　はなです。	9
	4. バードくんは　えいがを　みます。	10
の	1. バードくんは　たなかせんせいの　せいとです。	1
	2. これは　バードくんの　ノートです。	2
	3. これは　バードくんのです。	2
	4. にほんの　とけいです。	7
	5. 80えんの　きってを　ください。	7
	6. きのうの　ばん　テレビを　みました。	11
	7. パーティーの　まえに　はなを　かいます。	15
	8. べんきょうの　あとで　サッカーを　します。	15
か	1. アメリカじんですか。	1
	2. ちゅうごくじんですか、にほんじんですか。	1
	3. なんですか。	2
から	1. がっこうは　8じはんからです	3
	2. がっこうは　8じはんから　3じ40ぷんまでです。	3
	3. カナダから　にほんへ　きました。	12
	4. あしたは　どようびですから、がっこうは　12じまでです。	15
まで	1. ひるやすみは　1じはんまでです。	3
	2. ひるやすみは　12じはんから　1じはんまでです。	3
と	1. やすみは　どようびと　にちようびです。	4
	2. えんぴつと　けしゴムを　ください。	6
	3. バードくんは　かとうくんと　がっこうへ　いきます。	14
も	1. これも　3000えんです。	6
	2. はしも　ください。	6
	3. バードくんは　なにも　たべません。	14
	4. バードくんは　どこも　いきません。	14

Particles	Examples	Lesson
を	1. ハンバーガーを ください。	6
	2. おちゃを のみます。	10
	3. ファミコンを します。	10
で	1. 1000えんで おねがいします。	8
	2. ぜんぶで 480えんです。	8
	3. としょかんで ほんを よみます。	11
	4. じてんしゃで こうえんへ いきます。	13
	5. ひとりで いきます。	14
	6. べんきょうの あとで サッカーを します。	15
に	1. まいあさ 7じに おきます。	11
	2. にちようびに いきました。	11
	3. パーティーの まえに はなを かいます。	15
が	1. A : どの バスが いきますか。	12
	B : あの 1ばんの バスが いきます。	
	2. ときどき かんじが わかりません。	15
	3. ときどき かんじが わかりませんが、にほんごは おもしろいです。	15
へ	こうえんへ いきます。	12
や	パンや たまごを たべます。	15
ね	がっこうの でんわばんごうは 3785-2411ですね。	2
よ	きれいな まちですよ。	9

Mini Dictionary
ちいさいじしょ

Japanese-English Glossary with Kana Lookup

にほんご	English	Romaji	Lesson	Page
あ				
あ	ah	a	8	102
アイスクリーム	ice cream	aisukuriimu	7	87
あいだ	between	aida	15	192
あおい	blue	aoi	8	99
あかい	red	akai	8	95
あくしゅ	handshake	akushu	11	146
あくしゅを　した	shook hands	akushu o shita	11	146
あさ	morning	asa	10	117
あさごはん	breakfast	asa-gohan	11	144
あさって	the day after tomorrow	asatte	4	43
あした	tomorrow	ashita	4	43
あたらしい	new	atarashii	10	128
あとで	after	ato de	15	187
あに	my older brother	ani	5	53
あね	my older sister	ane	5	49
あの	that (over there)	ano	7	87
あぶない	dangerous, be careful	abunai	5	57
あまり…ません	not very…	amari…masen	15	192
アメリカ	America	Amerika	1	1
あるいて	on foot, walking	aruite	13	163
あれ	that, that one	are	6	63
い				
いい	good	ii	10	129
いいえ	no	iie	1	7
いかが	how	ikaga	9	114
いきます（いく）	go	ikimasu (iku)	12	151, 160
イギリス	England	Igirisu	1	7
いくつ	how many	ikutsu	7	87
いくら	how much	ikura	6	71
いす	chair	isu	2	19
いただきます	eat (polite word for tabemasu)	itadakimasu	9	114
イタリア	Italy	Itaria	7	87
いち	one	ichi	1	7
いちばん	No.1	ichi-ban	12	160
いちまん	ten thousand	ichi-man	7	87
いつ	when	itsu	5	53
いつか	fifth day of the month	itsuka	5	53
いつつ	five	itsutsu	7	87
いつも	always	itsumo	10	128

にほんご	English	Romaji	Lesson	Page
いっしょに	together	issho ni	10	130
いってきます	good-bye (said by person leaving)	itte kimasu	121	58
いってらっしゃい	good-bye (said by person staying)	itterasshai	121	58
いま	living room	ima	11	144
いま	now	ima	3	27
います（いる）	stay	imasu	15	187
いもうと	my younger sister	imōto	5	53
いもうとさん	(someone else's) younger sister	imōto-san	5	53
いらっしゃい	come in	irasshai	13	170
いらっしゃいませ	come in/welcome	irasshaimase	6	72
インド	India	Indo	1	7

う

うち	home	uchi	2	19
うみ	sea, ocean	umi	9	111
うん	um, un-huh, yeah (informal)	un	2	22

え

え	picture, drawing	e	9,10	112,128
えいが	movie, cinema	eiga	10	117
えいご	English language	Ē-go	4	43
ええと	let me see	ēto	3	34
えき	station	eki	12	157
えはがき	picture postcard	e-hagaki	9	112
〜えん	yen	-en	6	63

お

お〜	(prefix)	o-	6	71
おあがりください	please come in	o-agari kudasai	13	170
おいしい	good, delicious	oishii	9	114
おおきい	large, big	ōkii	8	95
オーストラリア	Australia	Ōsutoraria	1	7
おかあさん	mother, (someone else's) mother	okāsan	4,5	45,53
おかえりなさい	welcome back	o-kaerinasai	14	178
おかし	snacks (cakes, sweets, and savories)	o-kashi	9	114
おきた	woke up (informal speech for okimashita)	okita	11	146
おきます（おきる）	get up	okimasu (okiru)	11	135
おさけ	saké	o-sake	10	128
おじゃまします	sorry to intrude	o-jama shimasu	13	170
おすもうさん	sumo wrestler	o-sumō-san	11	146
おそくなって　すみません	I am sorry to be late	Osoku natte sumimasen	4	45
おちゃ	green tea, tea in general	o-cha	6	71
おてら	temple	o-tera	9	112
おとうさん	father, (someone else's) father	otōsan	1	10
おとうと	my younger brother	otōto	5	53
おとうとさん	(someone else's) younger brother	otōto-san	5	53
おとこ	man, male	otoko	7	90
おととい	the day before yesterday	ototoi	4	43
おにいさん	(someone else's) older brother	oniisan	5	53
おねえさん	(someone else's) older sister	onēsan	5	53
おはし	chopsticks	o-hashi	6	74
おべんとう	box lunch	o-bentō	6	74
おまちください	please wait	o-machi kudasai	8	100
おもしろい	interesting	omoshiroi	10	128
おんがく	music	ongaku	4	43
おんな	woman, female	onna	7	90

にほんご	English	Romaji	Lesson	Page
か				
か	=? (question marker, particle)	ka	1	1
が	(subject marker, particle)	ga	12	160
…が	…but (particle)	…ga	15	187
かいしゃ	company	kaisha	2	19
かいしゃいん	company employee	kaisha-in	1	10
かいます（かう）	buy	kaimasu (kau)	10	128
かいもの	shopping	kaimono	10	117
かいものを　します（かいものを　する）	shop	kaimono o shimasu kaimono o suru	10	117
かえります（かえる）	go back, return	kaerimasu (kaeru)	12	151
かきます（かく）	write	kakimasu (kaku)	10	128
かぎ	key	kagi	2	19
かさ	umbrella	kasa	11	144
カセット	cassette tape	kasetto	10	128
かぞく	family	kazoku	5	58
かたかな	katakana	katakana	10	128
～がつ	month	-gatsu	5	49
がっこう	school	gakkō	2	15
カナダ	Canada	Kanada	1	7
かばん	bag	kaban	2	19
かみ	paper	kami	6	71
カメラ	camera	kamera	11	144
かようび	Tuesday	ka-yōbi	4	43
から	from (particle)	kara	3, 12	27, 151
…から	because (particle)…	…kara	15	187
かわ	river	kawa	9	111
かんこく	Republic of Korea	Kankoku	12	157
かんじ	Chinese characters	Kanji	10	128
き				
ききます（きく）	listen	kikimasu (kiku)	10	128
きっさてん	coffee shop	kissaten	11	144
きのう	yesterday	kinō	4	39
きます（くる）	come	kimasu (kuru)	12	151
きゅう	nine	kyū	1	7
きょう	today	kyō	4	39
きょうしつ	classroom	kyōshitsu	11	144
きょうと	Kyoto (city and prefecture)	Kyōto	9	107
きょねん	last year	kyonen	12	151, 157
きれいな	pretty, beautiful, clean	kirēna	9	107
きを　つけて	take care	ki o tsukete	12	158
ぎんこう	bank	ginkō	12	157
ぎんざ	name of area in Tokyo	Ginza	11	144
きんようび	Friday	kin-yōbi	4	39
く				
く	nine	ku	1	7
くうこう	airport	kūkō	13	167
くすり	medicine	kusuri	10	128
ください	please (give me)	kudasai	6	63
くつ	shoes	kutsu	11	144
くるま	car	kuruma	2	19
くろい	black	kuroi	8	99
～くん	(suffix used when addressing younger men or boys)	-kun	1	1
け				
けさ	this morning	kesa	14	177

にほんご	English	Romaji	Lesson	Page
けしゴム	eraser	keshigomu	6	71
げつようび	Monday	getsu-yōbi	4	39
げんきな	healthy (not used for things), cheerful	genkina	9	111

こ

にほんご	English	Romaji	Lesson	Page
こ	child	ko	7	90
ご	five	go	1	7
～ご	language	-go	4	39
こうえん	park	kōen	9	111
こうちょう	principal	kōchō	1	8
コーヒー	coffee	kōhii	8	99
コーラ	cola	kōra	8	95
ごご	PM	gogo	3	31
ここのか	ninth day of the month	kokonoka	5	53
ここのつ	nine	kokonotsu	7	87
ごぜん	AM	gozen	3	31
ことし	this year	kotoshi	14	173
こども	child	kodomo	9	111
この	this	kono	7	79
ごはん	cooked rice	gohan	10	128
ごめんなさい	sorry	gomennasai	4	45
これ	this, this one	kore	2	15
ごろ	about	goro	12	158
コロラド	Colorado	Kororado	3	34
こんばん	this evening, tonight	komban	10	130

さ

にほんご	English	Romaji	Lesson	Page
～さい	-years old	-sai	5	49
さかな	fish	sakana	10	128
さくら	cherry blossoms	sakura	9	107
サッカー	soccer	sakkā	14	181
サッカーを します （サッカーを する）	play soccer	sakkā o shimasu sakkā o suru	14	181
サラダ	salad	sarada	8	99
さん	three	san	1	7
～さん	Mr., Mrs., Ms., Miss (honorific suffix)	-san	1	7
サンドイッチ	sandwich	sandoitchi	10	128

し

にほんご	English	Romaji	Lesson	Page
し	four	shi	1	7
～じ	o'clock	-ji	3	27
ＣＤ(シーディー)	compact disc	shiidii	10	128
しごと	work	shigoto	3	31
じしょ	dictionary	jisho	10	128
しずかな	quiet	shizukana	9	111
した	did (informal speech for shimashita)	shita	11	146
しち	seven	shichi	1	7
じてんしゃ	bicycle	jitensha	6	74
します	do	shimasu	10	117
しません	do not do	shimasen	10	117
じゃあ	well then	jā	6	72
しゃしん	photograph	shashin	7	90
シャツ	shirt	shatsu	7	87
じゅう	ten	jū	1	7
ジュース	juice	jūsu	8	99
じゅうどう	judo	jūdō	10	128
じゅうどうを します （じゅうどうを する）	do judo	jūdō o shimasu jūdō o suru	10	128

にほんご	English	Romaji	Lesson	Page
しゅくだい	homework	shukudai	10	128
しゅくだいを します（しゅくだいを する）	do one's homework	shukudai o shimasu shukudai o suru	10	128
しょうしょう	a moment	shōshō	8	100
ジョギング	jogging	jogingu	15	187
ジョギングを します（ジョギングを する）	jog	jogingu o shimasu jogingu o suru	15	187
しょくどう	cafeteria, canteen	shokudō	11	135
しろい	white	shiroi	8	99
～じん	person (suffix)	-jin	1	1
しんかんせん	"Shinkansen" Bullet train	Shinkansen	13	167
しんせつな	kind	shinsetsuna	9	111
しんぶん	newspaper	shimbun	2	19

す

スイス	Switzerland	Suisu	7	87
すいようび	Wednesday	sui-yōbi	4	43
すうがく	mathematics	sūgaku	4	43
スーパー	supermarket	sūpā	3	31
スープ	soup	sūpu	10	128
～すぎ	after	-sugi	15	192
すこし	a little	sukoshi	15	187
する	do	suru	10	117

せ

せいと	student, pupil	sēto	1	1
セーター	sweater	sētā	7	87
ゼロ	zero	zero	1	7
せん	one thousand	sen	4	43
せんげつ	last month	sen-getsu	12	157
せんしゅう	last week	sen-shū	12	157
せんせい	teacher	sensē	1	1
～せんせい	(honorific for a teacher)	-sensē	1	1
ぜんぜん…ません	not ever…	zenzen…masen	15	192
せんぱい	one's senior	sempai	14	177
ぜんぶで	in total	zenbu de	6	75

そ

そうじ	cleaning	sōji	3	31
そして	and then	soshite	12	158
その	that	sono	7	79
それ	that, that one	sore	6	63
それから	and	sorekara	7	88
そろばん	abacus	soroban	2	22

た

タイ	Thailand	Tai	12	157
たいいく	physical education	taiiku	4	43
たいいくかん	gymnasium	taiikukan	11	144
だいじょうぶ（な）	OK, all right	daijōbu (na)	5	57
たいてい	usually	taitē	11	146
たかい	expensive	takai	8	99
タクシー	taxi	takushii	13	167
ただいま	I'm back	tadaima	14	178
たべます（たべる）	eat	tabemasu (taberu)	10, 11	128, 146
たまご	egg	tamago	10	128
だれの	whose	dare no	2	19
たんじょうび	birthday	tanjōbi	5	49

にほんご	English	Romaji	Lesson	Page
ち				
ちいさい	small	chiisai	8	95
ちかてつ	subway, underground railway	chikatetsu	13	167
ちず	map	chizu	6, 10	71, 128
ちち	my father	chichi	5	49
～ちゃん	(suffix used when talking to children or close friends)	-chan	4	45
ちゅうごく	China	Chūgoku	1	7
つ				
ついたち	first day of the month	tsuitachi	5	53
つくえ	desk	tsukue	2	19
て				
で	at (particle)	de	11	135
で	by (particle)	de	13	163
～で おねがいします	please take it out of ¥～	-de o-negai shimasu	8	103
てがみ	letter	tegami	10	128
でした	was	deshita	4	39
です	is, will be	desu	1	1
ではありません	is not, will not be	dewa arimasen	1	1
ではありませんでした	was not	dewa arimasendeshita	4	39
デパート	department store	depāto	3	31
テレビ	television	terebi	10	128
でんしゃ	train	densha	13	167
でんち	battery	denchi	11	144
でんわ	telephone	denwa	2	15
でんわばんごう	telephone number	denwa-bangō	2	15
と				
と	and (particle)	to	4	39
ドイツ	Germany	Doitsu	7	87
どう いたしまして	don't mention it, you're welcome	dō itashimahshite	3	32
とうきょうえき	Tokyo Station	Tōkyō-Eki	11	146
とうきょうディズニーランド	Tokyo Disneyland	Tōkyō Dizuniirando	13	170
どうぞ	here you are	dōzo	6	72
どうぞ よろしく	I'm very glad to meet you.	dōzo yoroshiku	1	8
どうぶつえん	zoo	dōbutsuen	14	178
どうも ありがとうございました	thank you very much	dōmo arigatō gozaimashita	3	32
とお	ten	tō	7	87
とおか	tenth day of the month	tōka	5	53
ときどき	sometimes	tokidoki	10	117
とけい	watch, clock	tokē	2	15
どこ	where	doko	9	114
ところ	place	tokoro	9	111
どこの	of which country	doko no	7	87
どこも…ません	go …nowhere	doko mo…masen	14	173
としょかん	library	toshokan	11	144
とても	very	totemo	9	187
どなた	who (polite word for dare)	donata	7	90
どの	which	dono	7	90
ともだち	friend	tomodachi	1	7
どようび	Saturday	do-yōbi	4	39
どれ	which one	dore	6	74
どんな	what kind of	donna	9	107

にほんご	English	Romaji	Lesson	Page
まいあさ	every morning	maiasa	10	117
まいにち	every day	mainichi	10	128
まいばん	every evening, every night	maiban	10	128
～まえ	before	mae	15	192
まえに	before	mae ni	15	187
まだ	not yet	mada	13	170
まち	town, city	machi	9	107
まちます（まつ）	wait	machimasu	8	100
まで	until (particle)	made	3	27
まんが	comic	manga	10	128

み

みず	water	mizu	6	71
みせ	store, shop	mise	6	72
みせてください	please show me	misete kudasai	6	72
みた	saw (informal speech for mimashita)	mita	11	146
みっか	third day of the month	mikka	5	53
みっつ	three	mittsu	7	79
みましょう	let's watch	mimashō	10	130
みます（みる）	see	mimasu (miru)	10	117
ミルク	milk	miruku	8	99

む

むいか	sixth day of the month	muika	5	53
むっつ	six	muttsu	7	87

め

メニュー	menu	menyū	8	102

も

も	too, also (particle)	mo	6	63
もう	already	mō	13	170
もう	more	mō	8	102
もくようび	Thursday	moku-yōbi	4	39

や

や	…and … etc. (particle)	ya	15	187
やすい	cheap	yasui	8	99
やすみ	rest (period); vacation, holiday	yasumi	3, 5	27, 57
やっつ	eight	yattsu	7	87
やま	mountain	yama	9	111

ゆ

ゆうびんきょく	post office	yūbinkyoku	11	144
ゆうめいな	famous	yumēna	9	111

よ

よ	I tell you (particle)	yo	11	146
ようか	eighth day of the month	yōka	5	53
～ようび	day of the week	-yōbi	4	39
よく	often	yoku	10	128
よっか	fourth day of the month	yokka	5	53
よっつ	four	yottsu	7	87
よみます（よむ）	read	yomimasu (yomu)	10	128
よん	four	yon	1	7

ら

らいげつ	next month	rai-getsu	12	157

にほんご	English	Romaji	Lesson	Page
らいしゅう	next week	rai-shū	12	157
らいねん	next year	rai-nen	12	151

り
りか	science	rika	4	43

れ
れい	zero	rei	1	7
れきし	history	rekishi	4	43
レシート	receipt	reshiito	6	71
れんしゅう	practice	renshū	14	180
れんしゅうを　する	practice	renshū o suru	14	180

ろ
ろく	six	roku	1	7

わ
ワイン	wine	wain	7	87
わかります（わかる）	understand	wakarimasu (wakaru)	15	187
わたし	I	watashi	1	1
わたしの	my	watashi no	2	20
わるい	bad	warui	15	192

を
を	(object marker, particle)	o	6	63

Japanese-English Glossary with Romaji Lookup

Romaji	にほんご	English	Lesson	Page
A				
a	あ	ah	8	102
abunai	あぶない	dangerous, be careful	5	57
aida	あいだ	between	15	192
akai	あかい	red	8	95
akushu	あくしゅ	shaking hands	11	146
akushu o shita	あくしゅを　した	shook hands	11	146
amari…masen	あまり…ません	not very…	15	192
Amerika	アメリカ	America	1	1
ane	あね	my older sister	5	49
ani	あに	my older brother	5	53
ano	あの	that (over there)	7	87
aoi	あおい	blue	8	99
are	あれ	that, that one	6	63
aruite	あるいて	on foot, walking	13	163
asa	あさ	morning	10	117
asa-gohan	あさごはん	breakfast	11	144
asatte	あさって	the day after tomorrow	4	43
ashita	あした	tomorrow	4	43
atarashii	あたらしい	new	10	128
ato de	あとで	after	15	187
B				
baiku	バイク	motorbike	13	167
-ban	～ばん	number (counter)	2	19
ban	ばん	evening	10	128
ban-gohan	ばんごはん	dinner	11	144
bangō	ばんごう	number	2	15
basu	バス	bus	12	151
bengoshi	べんごし	lawyer	1	10
benkyō	べんきょう	study	3	31
benkyō o shimasu	べんきょうを　します	study	10	117
bideo	ビデオ	video	10	130
bijutsu	びじゅつ	art	4	43
boku	ぼく	I (informal male speech)	2	22
Burajiru	ブラジル	Brazil	1	7
byōin	びょういん	hospital	12	157
C				
-chan	～ちゃん	(suffix used when talking to children or close friends)	4	45
chichi	ちち	my father	5	49
chiisai	ちいさい	small	8	95
chikatetsu	ちかてつ	subway, underground railway	13	167
chizu	ちず	map	6, 10	71, 128
Chūgoku	ちゅうごく	China	1	7
D				
daijōbu (na)	だいじょうぶ（な）	OK, all right	5	57
dare no	だれの	whose	2	19
de	で	at (particle)	11	135

Romaji	にほんご	English	Lesson	Page
de	で	by (particle)	13	163
-de o-negai shimasu	〜で おねがいします	please take it out of ¥〜	8	103
denchi	でんち	battery	11	144
densha	でんしゃ	train	13	167
denwa	でんわ	telephone	2	15
denwa-bangō	でんわばんごう	telephone number	2	15
depāto	デパート	department store	3	31
deshita	でした	was	4	39
desu	です	is, will be	1	1
dewa arimasen	ではありません	is not, will not be	1	1
dewa arimasendeshita	ではありませんでした	was not	4	39
dō itashimahshite	どう いたしまして	don't mention it, you're welcome	3	32
do-yōbi	どようび	Saturday	4	39
dōbutsuen	どうぶつえん	zoo	14	178
Doitsu	ドイツ	Germany	7	87
doko	どこ	where	9	114
doko mo...masen	どこも…ません	go ...nowhere	14	173
doko no	どこの	of which country	7	87
dōmo arigatō gozaimashita	どうも ありがとうございました	thank you very much	3	32
donata	どなた	who (polite word for dare)	7	90
donna	どんな	what kind of	9	107
dono	どの	which	7	90
dore	どれ	which one	6	74
dōzo	どうぞ	here you are	6	72
dōzo yoroshiku	どうぞ よろしく	I'm very glad to meet you.	1	8

E

Romaji	にほんご	English	Lesson	Page
e	え	picture, drawing	9, 10	112, 128
e	へ	to (particle)	12	151
Ē-go	えいご	English language	4	43
e-hagaki	えはがき	picture postcard	9	112
ēga	えいが	movie, cinema	10	117
eki	えき	station	12	157
-en	〜えん	yen	6	63
ēto	ええと	let me see	3	34

F

Romaji	にほんご	English	Lesson	Page
famikon	ファミコン	computer game machine	10	128
famikon o shimasu	ファミコンを します	play computer games	10	128
firumu	フィルム	film	11	144
-fun	〜ふん	-minutes	3	31
fune	ふね	ship, boat	13	167
Furansu	フランス	France	7	87
futari	ふたり	two people	5	57
futatsu	ふたつ	two	7	87
futsuka	ふつか	second day of the month	5	53

G

Romaji	にほんご	English	Lesson	Page
...ga	…が	...but (particle)	15	187
ga	が	(subject marker, particle)	12	160
gakkō	がっこう	school	2	15
-gatsu	〜がつ	month	5	49
genkina	げんきな	healthy (not used for things), cheerful	9	111
getsu-yōbi	げつようび	Monday	4	39
ginkō	ぎんこう	bank	12	157
Ginza	ぎんざ	name of area in Tokyo	11	144
-go	〜ご	language	4	39
go	ご	five	1	7

Romaji	にほんご	English	Lesson	Page
gogo	ごご	PM	3	31
gohan	ごはん	cooked rice	10	128
gomennasai	ごめんなさい	sorry	4	45
goro	ごろ	about	12	158
gozen	ごぜん	AM	3	31

H

hachi	はち	eight	1	7
hagaki	はがき	postcard	9	112
haha	はは	my mother	5	53
hai	はい	yes; present (response in rollcall)	1; 4	7; 45
hajimemashite	はじめまして	How do you do?	1	8
hambāgā	ハンバーガー	hamburger	8	99
han	〜はん	half	3	27
hana	はな	flower	9	107
hatsuka	はつか	twentieth day of the month	5	53
hayai	はやい	early	11	146
hē	へえ	is that right?	11	146
heya	へや	room	11	144
hikōki	ひこうき	airplane	13	167
hiragana	ひらがな	hiragana	10	128
hiru	ひる	noon	3	27
hiru-gohan	ひるごはん	lunch	11	135
hiru-yasumi	ひるやすみ	lunch time	3	27
hito	ひと	person	6, 7	72, 90
hitori	ひとり	one person	5	57
hitori de	ひとりで	alone	14	173
hitotsu	ひとつ	one	7	87
Hokkaidō	ほっかいどう	name of island north of Honshu	13	167
-hon, -bon, -pon	〜ほん、ぼん、ぽん	(counter for long slender objects)	7	79
hon-ya	ほんや	bookstore	11	135
hyaku	ひゃく	hundred	3	31

I

ichi	いち	one	1	7
ichi-ban	いちばん	No.1	12	160
ichi-man	いちまん	ten thousand	7	87
Igirisu	イギリス	England	1	7
ii	いい	good	10	129
iie	いいえ	no	1	7
ikaga	いかが	how	9	114
ikimasu (iku)	いきます（いく）	go	12	151
iku	いく	go (informal speech for ikimasu)	12	160
ikura	いくら	how much	6	71
ikutsu	いくつ	how many	7	87
ima	いま	living room	11	144
ima	いま	now	3	27
imasu	います（いる）	stay	15	187
imōto	いもうと	my younger sister	5	53
imōto-san	いもうとさん	(someone else's) younger sister	5	53
Indo	インド	India	1	7
irasshai	いらっしゃい	come in	13	170
irasshaimase	いらっしゃいませ	come in/welcome	6	72
issho ni	いっしょに	together	10	130
isu	いす	chair	2	19
itadakimasu	いただきます	eat (polite word for tabemasu)	9	114
Itaria	イタリア	Italy	7	87
itsu	いつ	when	5	53

Romaji	にほんご	English	Lesson	Page
itsuka	いつか	fifth day of the month	5	53
itsumo	いつも	always	10	128
itsutsu	いつつ	five	7	87
itte kimasu	いってきます	good-bye	12	158
itterasshai	いってらっしゃい	good-bye	12	158

J

Romaji	にほんご	English	Lesson	Page
jā	じゃあ	well then	6	72
-ji	〜じ	o'clock	3	27
-jin	〜じん	person (suffix)	1	1
jisho	じしょ	dictionary	10	128
jitensha	じてんしゃ	bicycle	6	7
jogingu	ジョギング	jogging	15	187
jogingu o shimasu	ジョギングを　します	jog	15	187
jū	じゅう	ten	1	7
jūdō	じゅうどう	judo	10	128
jūdō o shimasu	じゅうどうを　します	do judo	10	128
jūsu	ジュース	juice	8	99

K

Romaji	にほんご	English	Lesson	Page
ka	か	=? (question marker, particle)	1	1
ka-yōbi	かようび	Tuesday	4	43
kaban	かばん	bag	2	19
kaerimasu (kaeru)	かえります（かえる）	go back, return	12	151
kagi	かぎ	key	2	19
kaimasu (kau)	かいます（かう）	buy	10	128
kaimono	かいもの	shopping	10	117
kaimono o shimasu	かいものを　します	shop	10	117
kaisha	かいしゃ	company	2	19
kaisha-in	かいしゃいん	company employee	1	10
kakimasu (kaku)	かきます（かく）	write	10	128
kamera	カメラ	camera	11	144
kami	かみ	paper	6	71
Kanada	カナダ	Canada	1	7
Kanji	かんじ	Chinese characters	10	128
Kankoku	かんこく	Republic of Korea	12	157
…kara	…から	because (particle)…	15	187
kara	から	from (particle)	3, 12	27, 151
kasa	かさ	umbrella	11	144
kasetto	カセット	cassette tape	10	128
katakana	かたかな	katakana	10	128
kawa	かわ	river	9	111
kazoku	かぞく	family	5	58
kesa	けさ	this morning	14	177
keshigomu	けしゴム	eraser	6	71
ki o tsukete	きを　つけて	take care	12	158
kikimasu (kiku)	ききます（きく）	listen	10	128
kimasu (kuru)	きます（くる）	come	12	151
kin-yōbi	きんようび	Friday	4	39
kinō	きのう	yesterday	4	39
kirēna	きれいな	pretty, beautiful, clean	9	107
kissaten	きっさてん	coffee shop	11	144
ko	こ	child	7	90
kōchō	こうちょう	principal	1	8
kodomo	こども	child	9	111
kōen	こうえん	park	9	111
kōhii	コーヒー	coffee	8	99
kokonoka	ここのか	ninth day of the month	5	53

Romaji	にほんご	English	Lesson	Page
kokonotsu	ここのつ	nine	7	87
komban	こんばん	this evening, tonight	10	130
kono	この	this	7	79
kōra	コーラ	coke	8	95
kore	これ	this, this one	2	15
Kororado	コロラド	Colorado	3	34
kotoshi	ことし	this year	14	173
ku	く	nine	1	7
kudasai	ください	please (give me)	6	63
kūkō	くうこう	airport	13	167
-kun	〜くん	(suffix used when addressing younger men or boys)	1	1
kuroi	くろい	black	8	99
kuruma	くるま	car	2	19
kusuri	くすり	medicine	10	128
kutsu	くつ	shoes	11	144
kyō	きょう	today	4	39
kyo-nen	きょねん	last year	12	151
kyōshitsu	きょうしつ	classroom	11	144
Kyōto	きょうと	Kyoto (city and prefecture)	9	107
kyū	きゅう	nine	1	7

M

Romaji	にほんご	English	Lesson	Page
machi	まち	town, city	9	107
machimasu	まちます（まつ）	wait	8	100
mada	まだ	not yet	13	170
made	まで	until (particle)	3	27
mae	〜まえ	before	15	192
mae ni	まえに	before	15	187
-mai	〜まい	(counter for thin, flat objects)	7	87
mai-	まい〜	every	10	117
maiasa	まいあさ	every morning	10	117
maiban	まいばん	every evening, every night	10	128
mainichi	まいにち	every day	10	128
manga	まんが	comic	10	128
menyū	メニュー	menu	8	102
mikka	みっか	third day of the month	5	53
mimashō	みましょう	let's watch	10	130
mimasu (miru)	みます（みる）	see	10	117
miruku	ミルク	milk	8	99
mise	みせ	store, shop	6	72
misete kudasai	みせてください	please show me	6	72
mita	みた	saw (informal speech for mimashita)	11	146
mittsu	みっつ	three	7	79
mizu	みず	water	6	71
mo	も	too, also (particle)	6	63
mō	もう	already	13	170
mō	もう	more	8	102
moku-yōbi	もくようび	Thursday	4	39
muika	むいか	sixth day of the month	5	53
muttsu	むっつ	six	7	87

N

Romaji	にほんご	English	Lesson	Page
namae	なまえ	name	2	20
nan no	なんの	what kind of	8	102
nan-ban	なんばん	what number	2	19
nan-bon	なんぼん	how many	7	87
nan-gatsu	なんがつ	which month	5	53

Romaji	にほんご	English	Lesson	Page
otōto	おとうと	my younger brother	5	53
otōto-san	おとうとさん	(someone else's) younger brother	5	53
ototoi	おととい	the day before yesterday	4	43

P

pan	パン	bread	7	87
pen	ペン	pen	6	71
Perū	ペルー	Peru	12	157
piza	ピザ	pizza	7	87
poteto	ポテト	fried potato, potato	8	95
-pun	～ぷん	-minutes	3	31
purezento	プレゼント	gift	14	181
purinto	プリント	print-out	8	102
pūru	プール	pool	12	157

R

rai-getsu	らいげつ	next month	12	157
rai-nen	らいねん	next year	12	151
rai-shū	らいしゅう	next week	12	157
rei	れい	zero	1	7
rekishi	れきし	history	4	43
renshū	れんしゅう	practice	14	180
renshū o suru	れんしゅうを　する	practice (informal speech for renshū o shimasu)	14	180
reshiito	レシート	receipt	6	71
rika	りか	science	4	43
roku	ろく	six	1	7$

S

-sai	～さい	-years old	5	49
sakana	さかな	fish	10	128
sakkā	サッカー	soccer	14	181
sakkā o shimasu	サッカーを　します	play soccer	14	181
sakura	さくら	cherry blossoms	9	107
-san	～さん	Mr., Mrs., Ms., Miss (honorific suffix)	1	7
san	さん	three	1	7
sandoitchi	サンドイッチ	sandwich	10	128
sarada	サラダ	salad	8	99
sempai	せんぱい	one's senior	14	177
sen	せん	one thousand	4	43
sen-getsu	せんげつ	last month	12	157
sen-shū	せんしゅう	last week	12	157
-sensē	～せんせい	(honorific for a teacher)	1	1
sensē	せんせい	teacher	1	1
sētā	セーター	sweater	7	87
sēto	せいと	student, pupil	1	1
shashin	しゃしん	photograph	7	90
shatsu	シャツ	shirt	7	87
shi	し	four	1	7
shichi	しち	seven	1	7
shigoto	しごと	work	3	31
shiidii	ＣＤ(シーディー)	compact disc	10	128
shimasen	しません	do not do	10	117
shimasu	します	do	10	117
shimbun	しんぶん	newspaper	2	19
Shinkansen	しんかんせん	"Shinkansen" Bullet train	13	167
shinsetsuna	しんせつな	kind	9	111
shiroi	しろい	white	8	99

Romaji	にほんご	English	Lesson	Page
shita	した	did (informal speech for shimashita)	11	146
shizukana	しずかな	quiet	9	111
shokudō	しょくどう	cafeteria, canteen	11	135
shōshō	しょうしょう	a moment	8	100
shukudai	しゅくだい	homework	10	128
shukudai o shimasu	しゅくだいを します	do one's homework	10	128
sōji	そうじ	cleaning	3	31
sono	その	that	7	79
sore	それ	that, that one	6	63
sorekara	それから	and	7	88
soroban	そろばん	abacus	2	22
soshite	そして	and then	12	158
sūgaku	すうがく	mathematics	4	43
-sugi	～すぎ	after	15	192
sui-yōbi	すいようび	Wednesday	4	43
Suisu	スイス	Switzerland	7	87
sukoshi	すこし	a little	15	187
sūpā	スーパー	supermarket	3	31
sūpu	スープ	soup	10	128
suru	する	do	10	117

T

Romaji	にほんご	English	Lesson	Page
tabemasu (taberu)	たべます（たべる）	eat	10	128
tadaima	ただいま	I'm back	14	178
Tai	タイ	Thailand	12	157
taiiku	たいいく	physical education	4	43
taiikukan	たいいくかん	gymnasium	11	144
taitē	たいてい	usually	11	146
takai	たかい	expensive	8	99
takushii	タクシー	taxi	13	167
tamago	たまご	egg	10	128
tanjōbi	たんじょうび	birthday	5	49
tegami	てがみ	letter	10	128
terebi	テレビ	television	10	128
to	と	and (particle)	4	39
tō	とお	ten	7	87
tōka	とおか	tenth day of the month	5	53
tokē	とけい	watch, clock	2	15
tokidoki	ときどき	sometimes	10	117
tokoro	ところ	place	9	111
Tōkyō Dizuniirando	とうきょうディズニーランド	Tokyo Disneyland	13	170
Tōkyō-Eki	とうきょうえき	Tokyo Station	11	146
tomodachi	ともだち	friend	1	7
toshokan	としょかん	library	11	144
totemo	とても	very	9	187
tsuitachi	ついたち	first day of the month	5	53
tsukue	つくえ	desk	2	19

U

Romaji	にほんご	English	Lesson	Page
uchi	うち	home	2	19
umi	うみ	sea, ocean	9	111
un	うん	um, un-huh, yeah (informal)	2	22

W

Romaji	にほんご	English	Lesson	Page
wa	は	as for (topic marker, particle)	1	1
wain	ワイン	wine	7	87
wakarimasu (wakaru)	わかります（わかる）	understand	15	187
warui	わるい	bad	15	192

Romaji	にほんご	English	Lesson	Page
watashi	わたし	I	1	1
watashi no	わたしの	my	2	20

Y

ya	や	...and ... etc. (particle)	15	187
yama	やま	mountain	9	111
yasui	やすい	cheap	8	99
yasumi	やすみ	rest (period); vacation, holiday	3, 5	27, 57
yattsu	やっつ	eight	7	87
yo	よ	I tell you (particle)	11	146
-yōbi	～ようび	day of the week	4	39
yōka	ようか	eighth day of the month	5	5
yokka	よっか	fourth day of the month	5	53
yoku	よく	often	10	128
yomimasu (yomu)	よみます（よむ）	read	10	128
yon	よん	four	1	7
yottsu	よっつ	four	7	87
yūbinkyoku	ゆうびんきょく	post office	11	144
yumēna	ゆうめいな	famous	9	111

Z

zenbu de	ぜんぶで	in total	6	75
zenzen...masen	ぜんぜん…ません	not ever...	15	192
zero	ゼロ	zero	1	7

English-Japanese Glossary

English	にほんご	Romaji	Lesson	Page
A				
abacus	そろばん	soroban	2	22
about	ごろ	goro	12	158
after	～すぎ；あとで	sugi; ato de	15	192,187
ah	あ	a	8	102
airplane	ひこうき	hikōki	13	167
airport	くうこう	kūkō	13	167
alone	ひとりで	hitori de	14	173
already	もう	mō	13	170
also (particle)	も	mo	6	63
always	いつも	itsumo	10	128
AM	ごぜん	gozen	3	31
America	アメリカ	Amerika	1	1
and	それから；(particle)と	sorekara; to	7, 4	88, 39
and then	そして	soshite	12	158
…and … etc. (particle)	や	ya	15	187
art	びじゅつ	bijutsu	4	43
as for (topic marker, particle)	は	wa	1	1
at (particle)	で；に	de; ni	11	135
Australia	オーストラリア	Ōsutoraria	1	7
B				
bad	わるい	warui	15	192
bag	かばん	kaban	2	19
bank	ぎんこう	ginkō	12	157
battery	でんち	denchi	11	144
beautiful	きれいな	kirēna	9	107
be careful	あぶない	abunai	5	57
because (particle)…	…から	…kara	15	187
before	まえに；～まえ	mae ni; mae	15	187, 192
between	あいだ	aida	15	192
bicycle	じてんしゃ	jitensha	6	74
big	おおきい	ōkii	8	95
birthday	たんじょうび	tanjōbi	5	49
black	くろい	kuroi	8	99
blue	あおい	aoi	8	99
boat	ふね	fune	13	167
bookstore	ほんや	hon-ya	11	135
box lunch	おべんとう	o-bentō	6	74
Brazil	ブラジル	Burajiru	1	7
bread	パン	pan	7	87
breakfast	あさごはん	asa-gohan	11	144
brother	(elder)おにいさん，(own)あに；(younger)おとうとさん，(own)おとうと	oniisan, ani; otōto-san, otōto	5	53
bus	バス	basu	12	151
…but (particle)	…が	…ga	15	187
buy	かいます（かう）	kaimasu (kau)	10	12
by (particle)	で	de	13	163

English	にほんご	Romaji	Lesson	Page
C				
cafeteria	しょくどう	shokudō	11	135
camera	カメラ	kamera	11	144
Canada	カナダ	Kanada	1	7
canteen	しょくどう	shokudō	11	135
car	くるま	kuruma	2	19
cassette tape	カセット	kasetto	10	128
chair	いす	isu	2	19
cheap	やすい	yasui	8	99
cheerful	げんきな	genkina	9	111
cherry blossoms	さくら	sakura	9	107
child	こ；こども	ko; kodomo	7; 9	90; 111
China	ちゅうごく	Chūgoku	1	7
Chinese characters	かんじ	Kanji	10	128
chopsticks	おはし	o-hashi	6	74
classroom	きょうしつ	kyōshitsu	11	144
clean	きれいな	kirēna	9	107
cleaning	そうじ	sōji	3	31
clock	とけい	tokē	2	15
coffee	コーヒー	kōhii	8	99
coffee shop	きっさてん	kissaten	11	144
coke	コーラ	kōra	8	95
Colorado	コロラド	Kororado	3	34
come	きます（くる）	kimasu (kuru)	12	151
come in	いらっしゃいませ； いらっしゃい	irasshaimase; irasshai	6; 13	72; 170
comic	まんが	manga	10	128
compact disc	ＣＤ(シーディー)	shiidii	10	128
company	かいしゃ	kaisha	2	19
company employee	かいしゃいん	kaisha-in	1	10
computer game machine	ファミコン	famikon	10	128
D				
day	(of the week)〜ようび； (of the month)〜にち	-yōbi; -nichi	4; 5	39; 49
day after tomorrow	あさって	asatte	4	43
day before yesterday	おととい	ototoi	4	43
delicious	おいしい	oishii	9	114
department store	デパート	depāto	3	31
desk	つくえ	tsukue	2	19
dictionary	じしょ	jisho	10	128
dinner	ばんごはん	ban-gohan	11	144
do	します（する）	shimasu (suru)	10	117
do judo	じゅうどうを　します （じゅうどうを　する）	jūdō o shimasu (jūdō o suru)	10	128
do not do	しません	shimasen	10	117
do one's homework	しゅくだいを　します （しゅくだいを　する）	shukudai o shimasu (shukudai o suru)	10	128
do... nothing	なにも…ません	nani mo...masen	14	177
drawing	え	e	10	128
drink	のみます（のむ）	nomimasu (nomu)	10	117
E				
early	はやい	hayai	11	146
eat	たべます（たべる）； (polite)いただきます	tabemasu (taberu); itadakimasu	10,11 9	128,146 114
egg	たまご	tamago	10	128
eight	はち；やっつ	hachi; yattsu	1; 7	7; 87

English	にほんご	Romaji	Lesson	Page
eighth day of the month	ようか	yōka	5	53
England	イギリス	Igirisu	1	7
English language	えいご	Ē-go	4	43
eraser	けしゴム	keshigomu	6	71
evening	ばん	ban	10	128
every	まい～	mai-	10	117
every day	まいにち	mainichi	10	128
every morning	まいあさ	maiasa	10	117
every night	まいばん	maiban	10	128
expensive	たかい	takai	8	99

F

English	にほんご	Romaji	Lesson	Page
family	かぞく	kazoku	5	58
famous	ゆうめいな	yumēna	9	111
father	おとうさん；(own)ちち	otōsan; chichi	1; 5	10; 45
female	おんな	onna	7	90
fifth day of the month	いつか	itsuka	5	53
film	フィルム	firumu	11	144
first day of the month	ついたち	tsuitachi	5	53
fish	さかな	sakana	10	128
five	ご；いつつ	go; itsutsu	1; 7	7; 87
flower	はな	hana	9	107
four	し，よん；よっつ	shi, yon; yottsu	1; 7	7; 87
fourth day of the month	よっか	yokka	5	53
France	フランス	Furansu	7	87
Friday	きんようび	kin-yōbi	4	39
fried potato	ポテト	poteto	8	95
friend	ともだち	tomodachi	1	7
from (particle)	から	kara	3, 12	27, 151

G

English	にほんご	Romaji	Lesson	Page
Germany	ドイツ	Doitsu	7	87
get up	おきます（おきる）	okimasu (okiru)	11	135
gift	プレゼント	purezento	14	181
go	いきます（いく）	ikimasu (iku)	12	151
go back	かえります（かえる）	kaerimasu (kaeru)	12	151
go to bed	ねます（ねる）	nemasu (neru)	11	144
go …nowhere	どこも…ません	doko mo…masen	14	173
good	いい；(delicious)おいしい	ii; oishii	10; 9	129; 114
good-bye	(said by person staying) いってらっしゃい；	itterasshai;	12	158
	(said by person leaving) いってきます	itte kimasu	12	158
green tea	おちゃ	o-cha	6	71
gymnasium	たいいくかん	taiikukan	11	144

H

English	にほんご	Romaji	Lesson	Page
half	～はん	han	3	2
hamburger	ハンバーガー	hambāgā	8	99
handshake	あくしゅ	akushu	11	146
here you are	どうぞ	dōzo	6	72
hiragana	ひらがな	hiragana	10	128
history	れきし	rekishi	4	43
holiday	やすみ	yasumi	5	57
home	うち	uchi	2	19
homework	しゅくだい	shukudai	10	128
hospital	びょういん	byōin	12	157
how	いかが	ikaga	9	114

English	にほんご	Romaji	Lesson	Page
How do you do?	はじめまして	hajimemashite	1	8
how many	いくつ；なんぼん；なんまい	ikutsu; nan-bon; nan-mai	7	87
how much	いくら	ikura	6	71
how old	なんさい	nan-sai	5	53
hundred	ひゃく	hyaku	3	31

I

English	にほんご	Romaji	Lesson	Page
I	わたし； (informal male speech) ぼく	watashi; boku	1, 2	1, 22
I'm back	ただいま	tadaima	14	178
ice cream	アイスクリーム	aisukuriimu	7	87
in total	ぜんぶで	zenbu de	6	75
India	インド	Indo	1	7
interesting	おもしろい	omoshiroi	10	128
is	です	desu	1	1
Italy	イタリア	Itaria	7	87

J

English	にほんご	Romaji	Lesson	Page
Japan	にほん	Nihon	1	7
Japanese language	にほんご	Nihon-go	4	39
jog	ジョギングを　します （ジョギングを　する）	jogingu o shimasu (jogingu o suru)	15	187
jogging	ジョギング	jogingu	15	187
judo	じゅうどう	jūdō	10	128
juice	ジュース	jūsu	8	99

K

English	にほんご	Romaji	Lesson	Page
katakana	かたかな	katakana	10	128
key	かぎ	kagi	2	19
kind	しんせつな	shinsetsuna	9	111
Kyoto (city and prefecture)	きょうと	Kyōto	9	107

L

English	にほんご	Romaji	Lesson	Page
language	～ご	-go	4	39
large	おおきい	ōkii	8	95
last month	せんげつ	sen-getsu	12	157
last week	せんしゅう	sen-shū	12	157
last year	きょねん	kyo-nen	12	151
lawyer	べんごし	bengoshi	1	10
let's watch	みましょう	mimashō	10	130
letter	てがみ	tegami	10	128
library	としょかん	toshokan	11	144
listen	ききます（きく）	kikimasu (kiku)	10	128
(a) little	すこし	sukoshi	15	187
living room	いま	ima	11	144
lunch	ひるごはん	hiru-gohan	11	135
lunch time	ひるやすみ	hiru-yasumi	3	27

M

English	にほんご	Romaji	Lesson	Page
man	おとこ	otoko	7	90
male	おとこ	otoko	7	90
map	ちず	chizu	5, 10	71, 128
mathematics	すうがく	sūgaku	4	43
meat	にく	niku	10	128
medicine	くすり	kusuri	10	128
menu	メニュー	menyū	8	102
milk	ミルク	miruku	8	99
-minutes	～ふん；～ぷん	-fun; -pun	3	31

English	にほんご	Romaji	Lesson	Page
(a) moment	しょうしょう	shōshō	8	100
Monday	げつようび	getsu-yōbi	4	39
month	〜がつ	-gatsu	5	49
more	もう	mō	8	102
morning	あさ	asa	10	117
mother	おかあさん；(own) はは	okāsan; haha	4; 5	45; 53
motorbike	バイク	baiku	13	167
mountain	やま	yama	9	111
movie, cinema	えいが	ēga	10	117
Mr., Mrs., Ms., Miss	〜さん	-san	1	7
music	おんがく	ongaku	4	43
my	わたしの	watashi no	2	20

N

English	にほんご	Romaji	Lesson	Page
name	なまえ	namae	2	20
new	あたらしい	atarashii	10	128
New Zealand	ニュージーランド	Nyūjirando	12	157
news	ニュース	nyūsu	10	128
newspaper	しんぶん	shimbun	2	19
next month	らいげつ	rai-getsu	12	157
next week	らいしゅう	rai-shū	12	157
next year	らいねん	rai-nen	12	151
nine	きゅう、く；ここのつ	kyū, ku; kokonotsu	1; 7	7; 83
ninth day of the month	ここのか	kokonoka	5	53
no	いいえ	iie	1	7
No.1	いちばん	ichi-ban	12	160
noon	ひる	hiru	3	27
not ever…	ぜんぜん…ません	zenzen…masen	15	192
not very…	あまり…ません	amari…masen	15	192
not yet	まだ	mada	13	170
notebook	ノート	nōto	2	19
now	いま	ima	3	27
number	ばんごう；(counter)〜ばん	bangō; -ban	2	15; 19

O

English	にほんご	Romaji	Lesson	Page
o'clock	〜じ	-ji	3	27
often	よく	yoku	10	128
OK	だいじょうぶ（な）	daijōbu (na)	5	57
on foot	あるいて	aruite	13	163
on (particle)	に	ni	11	135
one	いち；ひとつ	ichi; hitotsu	1; 7	7; 87
one person	ひとり	hitori	5	57

P

English	にほんご	Romaji	Lesson	Page
paper	かみ	kami	6	71
park	こうえん	kōen	9	111
pen	ペン	pen	6	71
person	ひと；(suffix)〜じん	hito; -jin	6, 7; 1	72, 90; 1
Peru	ペルー	Perū	12	157
photograph	しゃしん	shashin	7	90
physical education	たいいく	taiiku	4	43
picture	え	e	9	112
picture postcard	えはがき	e-hagaki	9	112
pizza	ピザ	piza	7	87
place	ところ	tokoro	9	111
play computer games	ファミコンを　します（ファミコンを　する）	famikon o shimasu (famikon o suru)	10	128

English	にほんご	Romaji	Lesson	Page
play soccer	サッカーを　します （サッカーを　する）	sakkā o shimasu (sakkā o suru)	14	181
please (give me)	ください	kudasai	6	63
please come in	おあがりください	o-agari kudasai	13	170
please show me	みせてください	misete kudasai	6	72
please wait	おまちください	o-machi kudasai	8	100
pm	ごご	gogo	3	31
pool	プール	pūru	12	157
postcard	はがき	hagaki	9	112
post office	ゆうびんきょく	yūbinkyoku	11	144
practice	れんしゅう	renshū	14	180
present (response in rollcall)	はい	hai	4	45
pretty	きれいな	kirēna	9	107
principal	こうちょう	kōchō	1	8
print-out	プリント	purinto	8	102

Q

English	にほんご	Romaji	Lesson	Page
quiet	しずかな	shizukana	9	111

R

English	にほんご	Romaji	Lesson	Page
read	よみます（よむ）	yomimasu (yomu)	10	128
receipt	レシート	reshiito	6	71
red	あかい	akai	8	95
Republic of Korea	かんこく	Kankoku	12	157
rest (period)	やすみ	yasumi	3, 5	27, 57
return	かえります（かえる）	kaerimasu (kaeru)	12	151
(cooked) rice	ごはん	gohan	10	128
river	かわ	kawa	9	111
room	へや	heya	11	144

S

English	にほんご	Romaji	Lesson	Page
saké	おさけ	o-sake	10	128
salad	サラダ	sarada	8	99
sandwich	サンドイッチ	sandoitchi	10	128
Saturday	どようび	do-yōbi	4	39
school	がっこう	gakkō	2	15
science	りか	rika	4	43
sea	うみ	umi	9	111
second day of the month	ふつか	futsuka	5	53
see	みます（みる）	mimasu (miru)	10	117
(one's) senior	せんぱい	sempai	14	177
seven	しち, なな；ななつ	shichi , nana; nanatsu	1; 7	7; 87
seventh day of the month	なのか	nanoka	5	53
"Shinkansen" Bullet train	しんかんせん	Shinkansen	13	167
ship, boat	ふね	fune	13	167
shirt	シャツ	shatsu	7	87
shoes	くつ	kutsu	11	144
shop	かいものを　します （かいものを　する）	kaimono o shimasu (kaimono o suru)	10	117
shopping	かいもの	kaimono	10	117
sister	(elder)おねえさん、(own)あね； (younger)いもうとさん、 (own)いもうと	onēsan, ane; imōto-san, imōto	5 5	53, 79 53
six	ろく；むっつ	roku; muttsu	1; 7	7; 87
sixth day of the month	むいか	muika	5	53
small	ちいさい	chiisai	8	95
snack	おかし	o-kashi	9	114
soccer	サッカー	sakkā	14	181

English	にほんご	Romaji	Lesson	Page
two	に；ふたつ	ni; futatsu	1; 7	7; 87
two people	ふたり	futari	5	57

U

English	にほんご	Romaji	Lesson	Page
umbrella	かさ	kasa	11	144
underground railway	ちかてつ	chikatetsu	13	167
understand	わかります（わかる）	wakarimasu (wakaru)	15	187
until (particle)	まで	made	3	27
usually	たいてい	taitē	11	146

V

English	にほんご	Romaji	Lesson	Page
vacation	やすみ	yasumi	5	57
very	とても	totemo	9	187
video	ビデオ	bideo	10	130

W

English	にほんご	Romaji	Lesson	Page
wait	まちます（まつ）	machimasu (matsu)	8	100
walking	あるいて	aruite	13	163
watch	とけい	tokē	2	15
water	みず	mizu	6	71
Wednesday	すいようび	sui-yōbi	4	43
welcome	いらっしゃいませ	irasshaimase	6	72
welcome back	おかえりなさい	o-kaerinasai	14	178
well then	じゃあ	jā	6	72
what	なん；なに	nan; nani	2	19; 22
what day of the week	なんようび	nan-yōbi	4	43
what kind of	なんの；どんな	nan no; donna	8; 9	102; 107
what number	なんばん	nan-ban	2	19
what time	なんじ	nan-ji	3	31
when	いつ	itsu	5	53
where	どこ	doko	9	114
which	どの	dono	7	90
which month	なんがつ	nan-gatsu	5	53
which day of the month	なんにち	nan-nichi	5	53
which one	どれ	dore	6	74
white	しろい	shiroi	8	99
who	どなた	donata	7	90
whose	だれの	dare no	2	19
wine	ワイン	wain	7	87
woman	おんな	onna	7	90
work	しごと	shigoto	3	31
write	かきます（かく）	kakimasu (kaku)	10	128

Y

English	にほんご	Romaji	Lesson	Page
-years old	～さい	-sai	5	49
yen	～えん	-en	6	63
yes	はい	hai	1	7
yesterday	きのう	kinō	4	39

Z

English	にほんご	Romaji	Lesson	Page
zero	れい；ゼロ	rei; zero	1	7
zoo	どうぶつえん	dōbutsuen	14	178

ヤングのための日本語　第1巻　スチューデントブック
JAPANESE FOR YOUNG PEOPLE I Student Book

1998年8月　第1刷発行
2009年8月　第12刷発行

著　者　　社団法人　国際日本語普及協会

発行者　　廣田浩二

発行所　　講談社インターナショナル株式会社
　　　　　〒112-8652　東京都文京区音羽 1-17-14
　　　　　電話　03-3944-6493（編集部）
　　　　　　　　03-3944-6492（営業部・業務部）
　　　　　ホームページ　www.kodansha-intl.com

印刷・製本所　　大日本印刷株式会社

にほんの　ちず

おきなわ

ひろしま

きょうと

ながさき

26

28

25

27

23

15

14

16

18

34

33

22

36

31

30

29

35

20

32

24

21

19

38

37

おおさか

なら